Praise for Er

"Stuck? Suffering from creat   y
familiar with Dr. Maisel's work need no introduction. ~~ ɔ a
psychotherapist and creativity coach who has made artists with
creative blocks his specialty. If you're creatively stuck, Maisel
uses common sense, exercises, and sound psychological techniques to get you unstuck."

— *Working Poet* on *Fearless Creating*

"Maisel's book has helpful suggestions for artists and writers
searching for encouragement and emotional respite."

— *Publishers Weekly* on *The Van Gogh Blues*

"Artists will appreciate Maisel's straightforward discussion of
the problems they face and his uplifting mantra of transcen-
dence and hope."

— *Variety* on *A Life in the Arts*

"A therapist who counsels creative and performing artists,
Maisel has fused his empirical knowledge of the artistic life
with true empathy and support for artists of all disciplines."

— *New Age Journal* on *A Life in the Arts*

"Eric Maisel speaks as the artist's friend and ally. He offers
powerful encouragement for people who undertake the courageous and often lonely adventure of finding, protecting, and
nourishing their creative voice."

— Stephen Nachmanovitch, author of *Free Play*,
on *A Life in the Arts*

"Eric Maisel has made a career out of helping artists, musicians,
dancers, and writers cope with the traumas and troubles that are
the price of admission to a creative life.... The author doesn't

just name and solve some common creative problems, he calls on us to create, and to create deeply. *Fearless Creating* mobilizes us to think, feel, and act completely, without self-editing and self-defeating restraint."

"Maisel suggests unique answers to the questions we face. I love this book and share it here at the outset of the year for artists and those who would be."

"Creativity coach, writer, and psychotherapist Eric Maisel has given us a simple, easy-to-use program to spur creativity and inspiration.... Often the ideas stay with me all day, firing me on to carry out my appointed tasks. The cards are not just for writers or artists but for anyone seeking to expand, explore, or open up channels of creativity. Highly recommended."

"Eric Maisel warrants special praise. He demonstrates unique sensitivity to the issues artists face and provides practical guidelines for artists whose mental health and creative outputs must be protected and promoted."

"Maisel intimately understands the anxieties of the creative process and the psychological landscape that artists inhabit. Strong on the psychology, Maisel is equally strong on practicalities.... What Maisel does, and does brilliantly, is explain how a book proposal can be not only a marketing tool but also an essential means for discovering what your book is about."

COACHING THE ARTIST WITHIN

Other Books by Eric Maisel

Fiction

The Blackbirds of Mulhouse
The Black Narc
Dismay
The Fretful Dancer
The Kingston Papers

Nonfiction

Affirmations for Artists
The Creativity Book
Deep Writing
Fearless Creating
Fearless Presenting
A Life in the Arts
Living the Writer's Life
Sleep Thinking
Staying Sane in the Arts
Ten-Second Centering
20 Communication Tips at Work
20 Communication Tips for Families
The Van Gogh Blues
Write Mind
A Writer's Paris

Journals

Artists Speak
Writers and Artists on Devotion
Writers and Artists on Love

Meditation Decks

Everyday Calm
Everyday Creative
Everyday Smart

COACHING THE ARTIST WITHIN

Advice for Writers, Actors,
Visual Artists & Musicians from
America's Foremost Creativity Coach

ERIC MAISEL

New World Library
Novato, California

New World Library
14 Pamaron Way
Novato, California 94949

Front cover design by Bill Mifsud
Text design and typography by Tona Pearce Myers

Library of Congress Cataloging-in-Publication Data
Maisel, Eric.
   Coaching the artist within : advice for writers, actors, visual artists, and musicians from America's foremost creativity coach / by Eric Maisel.—1st ed.
       p.   cm.
Includes index.
ISBN 1-57731-464-6 (pbk. : alk. paper)
1. Creative ability. 2. Creation (Literary, artistic, etc.)
3. Artists—Psychology. I. Title.
BF408.M232 2005
153.3'5—dc22   2004021427

First printing, January 2005
ISBN 1-57731-464-6

♻ Printed in Canada on 100% postconsumer waste recycled paper

🅖 A proud member of the Green Press Initiative

Distributed to the trade by Publishers Group West

10   9   8   7   6   5   4   3   2   1

For Ann,
twenty-eight years
into this adventure
and counting

CONTENTS

Appendix

INTRODUCTION

ne morning I get a call from John, a well-known musician who lives in Los Angeles. His band is falling apart. The drummer is back on heroin. The bassist is doing something criminal, dangerous, and stupid (though not drugs). The lead guitarist — this seems to make John the craziest — has taken to wearing a floppy hat on stage, a hat that John just can't stand. A hundred things in his life — no, two hundred — are a total mess. John runs through four of the two hundred — troubles with his girl-friend, troubles with his big house, troubles with his label, troubles with his manager.

"That's a lot to take in," I say.

"That's a lot to live," he replies.

"What do you want to do?" I ask him.

"Come to San Francisco and see you," he says.

We meet at my office — an out-of-the-way café with a quiet garden in the back. This is where I see clients. We talk for two hours. It turns out that what's actually on John's mind is that he hates the songs he's been writing. We focus on this. I ask him questions, listen to what he says, come to certain conclusions about what he really means and really wants to do.

"What about writing ballads about your childhood in Budapest?" I ask. "That might get at what you've been saying."

"That's exactly what I want to write!" he exclaims. "But I can't write those songs. The label would hate them. The band would hate them. Our fans would hate them. I haven't got an ounce of permission to write those songs."

I wait. He's thinking. I know that this is the moment John's been moving toward for months, maybe years. He needs a little nudge, a little encouragement.

"Do you want to write those songs?" I ask.

"I do," he replies in a small voice.

"Will you write those songs?"

"I will." It's barely a whisper.

"Start one right now."

"Right now? Here?"

"Here. I'll get us refills. Just begin."

He looks skeptical — but also willing. He jots a note on

the pad in front of him. He makes another note. Suddenly he looks around. It's an only-in-San-Francisco moment. In parts of San Francisco not much has changed since the sixties, and there on the bench across from us are a couple of leathery-skinned blues musicians, guitars in tow. My client gets up from our table, chats with them for a minute, and borrows one of their guitars. By the time I return with our coffee, John has a song written. It becomes the seventh track on his next album, an album that everyone proclaims to be the band's most poignant and lyrical.

Later that morning I get my weekly call from a best-selling novelist in England. Her house has more windows than my flat has books, and she has at her behest the kind of help you only encounter in English novels: gardeners, a personal assistant, a driver, specialty physicians who provide her with exercise and nutrition regimens, an astrologer, a masseuse. She has written a zillion genre novels. But she feels like a fraud because she's never tackled a single novel that she considers worthy. She claims she wants to tackle a novel of this sort — she even has one in mind — but she has set up her life so that deadlines for new novels arrive every four or five months. Then there are the publicity demands associated with each new novel. She's managed to allow herself absolutely no time or space to begin her "real work."

Margaret is aware that this unfortunate routine has to do with her fear that she isn't really capable of doing great work. She also knows that this fear is connected to childhood experiences of abandonment. She has excellent insight into her situation and in fact often acts as a lay therapist for her friends. But when Margaret tries to get near her "worthy novel," something like a hurricane rises up in her, causing all sorts of mayhem — accidents, legal assaults, crises with her children. She has a strong notion that the gods are demanding that she do great work and also that they are mocking her and preventing her from starting. She is their beloved at the same time that she is loathsome in their eyes.

We work on this issue, as we do every week, in the intimacy of a phone conversation. There is no more intimate coaching work than phone coaching. My clients who reside in London, Paris, New York, or Los Angeles are only a breath away, a millimeter away, as close as a person can be. In the course of our chat Margaret mentions the (very large) sum that her latest novel has made in its Swedish translation. It is more than I have made from a lifetime of writing.

"They love me in Sweden," she says.

We laugh.

"More than you love yourself," I murmur.

"Infinitely more than I love myself," she agrees.

"That'll be our work for the next fifteen minutes. All right?"

"I can feel the hurricane rising up already."

"Breathe, Margaret."

"I know this is the work. All right."

"You have worthy novels in you. Do you believe me?"

"I love it that you believe it. But I don't know if I believe it."

"Take that as your affirmation. All right? 'I have worthy novels in me.'"

"I have worthy novels in me."

"What are you feeling?"

"Like I'm going to die."

We sit with her terror for several seconds. Then we resume, two intelligent mortals taxed beyond all reckoning by the task of healing this wounded writer. It is the hardest of all labors, birthing a worthy book from a woman who doubts that she can deliver. When the hour is done I reheat my coffee and sit by the window for a moment, looking out at my corner of San Francisco Bay. The vista is framed on the left by a distant Mount Diablo and on the right by Candlestick Park. A mockingbird is singing.

In the early afternoon I drive to a local music conservatory and give a performance anxiety workshop for young opera singers. I teach them a special anxiety management tool I've been developing, called the Centering Sequence — a six-breath, six-thought, one-minute calming exercise. Then I have them stand, one by one, and silently sing arias to themselves. At a certain point I interrupt the current silent singer, whose anxiety is palpable.

"What's on your mind right now?" I ask.

"The D above high C that's coming soon," she replies.

"Do you feel prepared for it?"

"No!"

"But you usually hit it?"

"I hit it. But it's never beautiful."

"It'll be beautiful if you can just relax. You can add two

or three beautiful notes to either end of your range if you're more relaxed. Did you know that?"

"I've heard people say that. But it has no real meaning for me."

"Okay. You're going to practice the relaxation technique I taught you earlier. Then you're going to sing out loud. All right?"

"Bloody hell."

She runs through her warm-ups. I walk her through the Centering Sequence, and she sings. She hits her high notes beautifully. The young opera singers in the room are more than impressed: they are instantly motivated. We spend the rest of the time practicing the Centering Sequence and learning a few additional techniques. They chuckle when I teach them a personal favorite, silent screaming.

That evening my wife and I visit the Wild Side West, our local pub, a lesbian-but-hetero-tolerant bar with a fantasy back garden of toad-shaped benches, ruined pagodas, and leafy drinking niches. We catch up. Ann is a high school administrator and has many stories to tell. I tell her about the opera singers and the tricky turn my current nonfiction book is taking. We chat about our daughters, about recaulking the tub, about the possibility that we're eating too much fish. I give her the celery out of my Bloody Mary, which is no idle gesture, as we both love that celery.

At six the next morning I'm at my computer writing. I write every morning, seven days a week, for at least an hour and on good days for three or four. I try to sell the idea of regularity and routine to my clients, the idea that some significant percentage of the disappointment they feel about not creating will evaporate like sun-kissed mist if only they will commit to getting to their creative work first thing every morning. Creating should come first, absolutely first, before their yoga, before their mental chatter begins, before they start dressing for work or hauling the kids off to school. If they could only bring their "new-morning" mind to their creative work, they would work like angels. This is one of my coaching mantras.

At nine I have a phone client, an ex-pat painter who lives and works in Mexico City. She has the oddest problem, which actually isn't so odd at all. Six months ago she finished the largest project of her life, an enormous mural painted on the side of a church. She had a huge grant and several helpers. The project was so large that it took them a full six months just to prepare the wall for painting. The mural was a great success. She can hardly explain how good it felt to complete it and what pride she takes in the accomplishment. But since the day she finished the mural she hasn't been able to return to her studio. Her normal-sized canvases now bore her to tears.

Our work is to help her love painting in the studio again. Part of the problem, it turns out, is that she is tired of her old imagery. Returning to the studio feels deadly dull on two scores: the canvases feel too small, and the subject matter feels trivial. She has become quite well known for Mexico City cityscapes that are close to touristy, full of whimsy — or is it irony? — and that are incredibly popular with collectors. It has taken a few sessions, but today we arrive at the truth of the matter. She wants to go fully abstract, to pour her passion, wildness, and, yes, her despair and destructiveness into her canvases. She wants to break out of the jail of her customary imagery.

She's been holding the mural as both a blessing and a curse, staggeringly wonderful to have done but a stake driven into her normal way of working. Today we see it for what it was, completely a blessing. It has given her a powerful push in the direction she has long wanted to go. It's time for her to make enormous abstract paintings, even though her collectors will be horrified. Or will they? We agree that we don't know. We agree that it's impossible to say. We agree that, really, there is nothing to fear. She is excited, too excited to keep talking. We stop ten minutes early. Four hours later I get an email from her, telling me that her first abstract painting is now finished.

One of the things I've done during those four hours is read lesson responses from the creativity-coaches-in-training whom I'm grooming. Twice a year I initiate a sixteen-week training that draws about twenty aspiring creativity coaches. They live in the Netherlands, New Zealand, Israel, Singapore, Switzerland, rural and urban America, everywhere and anywhere that email reaches. In turn, they work with clients who themselves are flung all over the globe. The world has never seen anything like it. A coach-in-training in rural Georgia can work with a painter in Brazil, a rapper in New York, a poet in Berlin, and an architecture student a long stone's throw away in Savannah.

I find their responses poignant. They are just learning how to coach others, and they are also just learning how to coach themselves. What they are learning — about negative self-talk as a creativity killer, about the necessity of creating "in the middle of things," about the virtues of plans and schedules and baby steps — is eye-opening for them and is inspiring them to create. This is something of a problem for them, because they need to devote the little spare time they have to their work with clients. What I know will happen is that a substantial number of these coaches-in-training will experience an amazing burst of creativity as soon as the training ends. Though this was not their goal when they signed on — they thought they were investigating a new career option — it is an entirely welcome by-product of paying attention to how the creative process actually works.

In the afternoon I meet a client who's driven two hundred miles from Santa Barbara for our meeting at my "office." He is a successful (though not wildly successful) abstract painter whose canvases sell for $10,000 apiece and who, in good times, sells ten or more canvases annually out of his trendy Santa Barbara gallery, which his wife manages. I learn as we chat that he wants two contradictory things, to become a painter whose new paintings bring in $30,000 apiece and to stop painting altogether and become, at the age of fifty-five, a sculptor.

He is new to sculpting and is making many messes and mistakes. He is also new to the fabrication process and is finding it hard to rely on others. In his mild paranoia he feels that others, who happen to be less successful painters toiling away as fabricators, are actively sabotaging his sculptures. He is also worried (or rather his wife is worried) that sculpting is a grave indulgence, considering that they have bills to pay, including stunning ones for a new painting studio addition to his seaside home. Despite these caveats, he wants to sculpt. The problem isn't exactly that he's tired of painting, although that's part of it. More to the point is that his style of painting no longer challenges him, whereas everything about sculpting does.

In fact, he is looking for permission from me to be an artist. He wants to hear that I understand why he wants to sculpt and that I think he ought to sculpt. I freely grant him that permission — but not without first marching him step-by-step through the minefields, through the real conflicts, within him and between him and his wife, that are preventing him from committing to sculpture. Each conflict carries weight and must be addressed. Is it right to embark on something that will have a financial impact not only on him but on his wife? Is it wise to abandon painting entirely in this, the first blush of enthusiasm for sculpting? Is there a smart way both to paint and sculpt? These are the matters we address as a breeze rustles leaves and shifts shadows around us.

Later that afternoon I have an initial phone session with a woman who is working on her first novel. Jessica has worked on this novel sporadically for four years and is very disappointed in herself for making so little progress, for stumbling along without much energy or enthusiasm on a project she once thought she loved. She announces that she should probably be out making money, which her lawyer husband would dearly love her to earn, at some job or other rather than wasting so much time brooding about her novel. She hates feeling like a dilettante, a wannabe, a fool, and a failure.

I ignore her angst and interrogate her about what I need to know: what about this novel isn't working, what about it could work, and, if it is dead in the water, what novel might she try next. I conclude that Jessica is writing her novel about a failed marriage in too distanced and defended a way. She will only be able to continue if she can abandon her defensive distancing and bravely explore the roiling — and painful — dramas that led to the marriage's demise.

Jessica's desire to do "stylish work" has been a cover-up, a way to justify pretty paragraphs in which neither the husband nor the wife feel a thing. I tell Jessica this with the care and compassion that a coach must take when he or she communicates hard truths. And these truths are not even that hard when communicated in the right way. Jessica is enormously relieved to know why her novel hasn't been working — for she entirely agrees with my assessment. It suddenly comes to her how she might do the book differently. She is excited and a little sick to her stomach. We run over by fifteen minutes, which is no problem. I'm not watching the clock.

As a creativity coach, I get to help people create. I love doing this work — which brings me to the purpose of this book. I want to teach you how to become a more effective creator by guiding you through twelve self-coaching lessons. My hope is that by the end of these twelve lessons you will have become your own in-house expert, ready, willing, and able to deal with the challenges that the creative life brings. Following the program I've prepared for you means doing some exercises and bravely reflecting on underlying issues.

Each lesson comes with at least two exercises. Please give them a try — the rewards are truly tremendous! There's really no substitute for doing. If you engage with the exercises you'll find yourself growing dramatically as a creativity self-coach. You'll learn how to get new creative projects started, how to jump-start stalled projects, how to work deeply and without distraction on your current project, and how to handle the ups and downs of the creative journey. I think not only that you'll gain a great deal from tackling the exercises but also that you will love the experience.

For a more complete self-coaching program I recommend that you use *Coaching the Artist Within* in conjunction with the other books that I've written on the creative process and the creative life — I've listed them in the resources section at the back of the book. In those books you'll learn principles to help you create more regularly and deeply, strategies for handling creative anxiety, techniques for effectively meeting the art marketplace, and pointers on tackling problems like artistic depression, performance anxiety, and creative blockage. Those books, in conjunction with this one, will provide a more complete picture of the joys and troubles that await you as a creative person.

To spice up this journey I'll throw in some more secrets from the annals of a working creativity coach (while changing names and altering indentifying information). In the second part of each chapter, I'll take you with me to Paris, London, New York, or some other venue where I work. Ready to come along? In that case — bon voyage!

COACHING THE ARTIST WITHIN

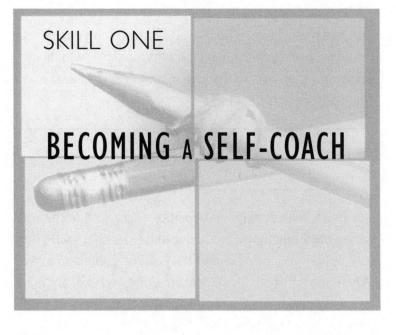

SKILL ONE

BECOMING a SELF-COACH

The ability to effectively coach yourself hinges on your having enough space to positively influence yourself, to openly communicate with yourself, to carefully monitor yourself, and to regularly chat with yourself. This mindful and ultimately courageous way of being requires that you get some distance from yourself, becoming a witness to your own life, birthing someone who compassionately but unflinchingly notices your antics and your defensive maneuvers and who, from the vantage point of an observer who has a little cultivated distance, motivates you, congratulates you, chides you when you need chiding, and loves you when you need loving.

This is the first skill we'll practice, separating yourself into two parts, your ordinary self (with which you are very familiar) and your "inner creativity coach" (which may prove a revelation). To that end, please try your hand at the following exercise.

EXERCISE 1

Chatting with Yourself

Get two kitchen chairs and position them so that they are facing each other. You are about to have a chat with yourself. When you sit in chair one you are going to be you. When you sit in chair two you are going to be your "inner creativity coach." It's as simple as that. Pick an issue that's been on your mind such as:

- not finishing your novel
- hating your day job but seeing no way out
- having doubts about your paintings' subject matter
- wanting to perform but suffering from performance anxiety
- tackling your anorexia
- being deeply, pervasively bored
- wanting to make documentary films but not feeling up to the challenge

I think you can see that this first step is magnificent and profound — finding the courage to confess to a real problem. We do this only rarely. We may suffer the fleeting thought "I am not finishing my novel" fifty times a day without once stopping to acknowledge or confess to the problem. We refuse to stop because we believe that stopping would make us incredibly anxious and ultimately result in a blow to our self-esteem.

We fear that if we stopped to confess we would drown in despair and self-loathing. So we needle and belittle ourselves while simultaneously doing nothing to solve the problem. What we must do is to fearlessly acknowledge the problem. This is what you do in chair one. You sit there and say to your coach, "I am not working on my novel. There. I've said it."

Then you move to chair two and play the role of coach. What do you reply as your own coach? It can be something in the spirit of inquiry, something obvious like, "Why aren't you writing? You claim that your novel is damned important to you, so what's going on?" This inquiry is a vital second step in the process. You-as-coach are interested in the "why" of the matter, just as an inventor is interested in knowing what filament works best in a lightbulb. You sit there prepared to figure out what's going on. You are going to bring everything you know about human nature and the realities of living to the encounter for the sake of getting to the bottom of the matter and finding a way out.

Now you return to chair one, since a question is pending.

Reseated in chair one, you mutter, "Why? Because the novel is shit." Now you must return to chair two instantly! If you don't, you'll wallow in that characterization, hate yourself and your novel, and be at exactly the same place you usually find yourself, paralyzed and without hope.

Back in chair two you continue: "So you say it's no good. First we need to figure out what that means. Is the novel's conception faulty? Is it really as boring and undramatic as you fear? Or does it just need more drafts and revisions? Golly, we certainly know how many revisions a novel might require! Have we forgotten that? — or do we think that we should be spared the task of revising? Or is it that it must be radically redone? — yes, I know how much work that would be! First of all, is your appraisal even correct? Do we need to show bits of it to Mike and Jane and see what other people think? We've certainly been avoiding doing that. What do you think?"

You can see that the basic requirements for becoming a coach are courage and common sense. As your own coach you ask yourself the most obvious questions and then try to answer them. You enter into real dialogue, you scratch your head, you try things out, you bat the issue back and forth. Virtually no one does this, even though it is clearly one of the best ways to proceed. How many times have you entered into real dialogue with the part of you that could coach you out of your difficulties? Today, if you are willing to do this exercise, the answer is, at least once.

Continue moving between the two chairs until you can honestly say that you've faithfully examined the issue you broached. Let an hour or two pass and then try the exercise again, this time without the chairs. Present an issue to your coach and coach yourself to an answer. Begin an everlasting coaching partnership with this simple exercise.

When you can't step away from yourself to observe, when you are boxed into yourself, your sight is myopic and your thinking repetitive and stereotypic. You can't see answers; in fact, you can't even see questions. Those thoughts and behaviors that do not serve you — calling yourself bad names, not creating, wresting illusory control by bingeing and purging or running marathons — become the only thoughts and behaviors available to you. You become a one-note wonder and the largeness of the universe cannot manifest itself in you. In this very common state you can't carry on a simple conversation with yourself, a conversation that might begin, "Eric, you haven't been writing recently. Let's chat about that without getting all anxious and defensive."

Acquiring this coach-inside, this compassionate witness, this round-the-clock friendly companion and taskmaster, is important beyond reckoning. Without this coach-inside, you are three-quarters blind. You make decisions only because you are feeling anxious and need to decide something. You spend years neither articulating nor fulfilling your life mission. You remain stubbornly uncoachable, someone who takes pride in his or her own small, faulty ways of doing things. It is one thing to reject the coaching of others —

that can certainly be wise. But to reject your own counsel? That has to be very close to cowardice.

The first self-coaching skill you must acquire is the willingness to bravely become your own coach. If you are not willing to take a radical new stance, to have conversations with yourself rather than shutting your mind to your own good thoughts — out of fear, doubt, and anxiety — you will not be able to master the other eleven skills I want to teach you. You don't need to take a formal coaching course — you already know everything you need to know. What you need is the *willingness* to coach yourself.

Perhaps you are deeply resistant to this process because of what it entails. It means exposing your cherished defenses and favorite excuses to the scrutiny of a second voice that says, "I love you, but no more bullshit." It means taking responsibility for what is in your control, not for wars and famine, not for overpopulation and a shrinking ozone layer, not for your father's temper and your day job's lousy vacation policy, but for how you will make meaning and for when and where you will create.

Most people never achieve this level of self-awareness, self-communication, and real courage. As a consequence they never become wise about their own motives, methods, and madnesses. They succumb to their depression and anxiety, soothe themselves by shopping or watching sports, and let decades pass in a trance. This is the common way, the entirely human way, the way that most people live, including those who have the itch to create.

This enormous first task, *finding the willingness to become your own coach,* really means finding the willingness to be truthful and objective about your situation and then doing whatever your situation requires, including things you don't want to do. There is simply no one else who can do this witnessing and coaching for you. A coach can't hit and field for his players. Each player must be her own self-coach if she is to throw to the right base and not swing at balls out of the strike zone. Your job today — and you can do it in five minutes flat, but only if you are willing — is to internalize a self-coaching voice, to say to yourself, "I am going to grow aware of my own antics and become my own unflinching friend, guide, and advocate."

This is not like activating your "inner stockbroker," "inner masseuse," "inner herbalist," or "inner real estate agent." This is the largest existential task confronting you, taking responsibility for the way you operate, the way you make meaning. Hiring on your inner creativity coach is the equivalent of saying, "I am ready to step up to the plate." You can do this only if your reasons for creating make sense to you. Why step to the plate if your potential paintings, songs, or poems — even the most profound and beautiful ones — don't really matter to you? The next exercise will help you discern what *does* matter to you.

<table>
<tr><td>EXERCISE 2</td></tr>
<tr><td>Deciding to Matter</td></tr>
</table>

Your ability to create is intimately connected to your intention to matter. If you don't really think that you, your ideas, or your work matter, you won't have the motivational juice to create. So I would like you to say, "I intend to matter" or, "My creative work matters," or "I matter" twenty or thirty times today. Will you do that? Start right now by saying "I matter" loud enough for me to hear you here in San Francisco. Keep saying "I matter" out loud and without embarrassment, until something clicks and you feel a steely resolve to be of significance.

Your first self-coaching skill is accepting the mantle of self-coach. Accepting this mantle is a learned skill — it is absolutely not automatic. In fact, this process runs counter to our habitual ways of dealing with things. If you learn to accept this mantle, then when something comes up — when *anything* comes up — instead of exclaiming, "Oh, hell!" or, "How disappointing!" or, "There I go again!" you stop, breathe, and say, "Let me coach myself through this situation." I don't expect that you'll learn this skill in a day, but I do hope that you'll at least consider beginning. Start right now by airing an important issue for you and your self-coach to consider.

Rising Sun, Indiana

I am in Rising Sun, Indiana, to give a keynote address and some workshops at the fledgling Rising Sun Writers Conference, which, it turns out, will be held at a middle school and will prove to be sorely underattended. The organizers have underestimated how long it takes to put together a writers' conference and have bravely tried to accomplish the feat in a few short months. As a result there are almost as many presenters as participants.

I am lodged at a waterside inn down a dirt road past the golf course. Outside my window rain is falling on the Ohio River. The river is much cleaner these days than in years past, and otter and beaver have returned in significant numbers. It is a beautiful spot, Indiana here, Kentucky there, forested glens, almost-extinct waterfowl, fertile, cultivated land on either bank diving right to the water's edge. The owners of the inn sport his-and-her Harleys and run off whenever they can for thousand-mile rides. An October rain falls, a harbinger of snows and winter. Coal barges drift down the river. The gambling boats that recently plied the Ohio have permanently moored at places with names like Aurora and Rising Sun, and resorts have sprung up on the shore beside them. Gambling money has given Rising Sun a new lease on life, and artists have been attracted here, to what was (and still is) a poor town in the poorest county in Indiana. Their numbers have increased so much that this year they organized the Rising Sun Writers Conference.

Last night at the conference reception I talked to several would-be writers who wished they could get their books going. Would they? Probably not. It wasn't that they couldn't write or didn't have the time. Rather, it was that they lacked that special internalized voice, that inner creativity coach, to help them weather the creative process and the fiery crucible of trial and error. They needed that spunky, sensible observer-cheerleader-taskmaster to provide simple advice like, "Write a first book and, if you don't like it, write a second book." They desperately needed their own help and guidance.

Why hadn't they hired that inner coach on? If the answer was fear, it wasn't fear in any ordinary sense. These would-be writers weren't cowards. They had survived divorces, sculpted with chain saws, raised children with severe disabilities. But despite their everyday courage, the courage to create eluded them.

I knew that what they feared was opening up a frightening can of worms. The sheer number of these anxiety-inducing issues overwhelmed them before they could even start. They feared their own intractable personalities, the hard work of creating, the art marketplace, and, above all else, core issues of meaning. To write would be to look meaning square in the eye. Dreadful, really! Fearing all this, they shut their minds to their own wisdom. This fear and its resultant lack of self-relationship made them feel downright stupid.

As a case in point, last night a participant at the conference, a woman of about thirty, came up to me, thrust out her hand, and introduced herself by saying, "Hello, I'm a dummy!" You think I'm making this up, but I'm not. I've heard some variation of this self-indictment more times than I can count. "Hi, I have no talent!" "Hi, I'm not really a painter!" "Hi, I haven't a thought in my head!" People really do shake my hand and say these horrible things.

I looked her in the eye and replied, "Never say that

again." She laughed, but something registered. We went off into a corner and talked. Her name was Melissa, she worked in a health food store, and she was chronically depressed. Naturally! Who wouldn't be severely depressed if her internal organization, her view of herself and her chances in life, caused her to introduce herself in that way? Just as naturally, she claimed to have no idea what book she might write; she had only this itch — an itch beyond scratching — to write something. There, in the corner, I coached her.

I asked her the simplest question: "What are you hoping to write?" There's nothing at all mysterious about the questions a creativity coach asks, any more than there is anything mysterious about the questions a doctor asks, like, "Where does it hurt?" and, "How long have you been running a fever?" When you act as your own coach, these are exactly the sorts of questions you'll ask yourself.

"I want to do a book about a famous dancer," she confessed.

"Any particular dancer?"

"No. I don't know who."

"You mean a novel? Or a biography?"

"A biography. I think."

"Man or woman?"

"Woman!"

"Because her life would be interesting and yours isn't?"

In the world of psychotherapy a comment of this sort has two names. It is called an interpretation and also an intervention. You wager a guess — an interpretation. You don't make this guess idly. You want to get something big on the table, something you consider vital for the person across from you to hear. You boldly and consciously "intervene" in that person's life, wagering not only your interpretation but also that you have said what you needed to say gently and well enough that it won't provoke too defensive a reaction.

Any sensible human being can ask a right first question of the "where does it hurt?" variety. It takes more experience and understanding to know what to say next, because what you say next is the equivalent of saying, "Sounds like appendicitis" or, "Sounds like gas." It also takes some daring, because no matter how gently or carefully you have framed your comment, it's likely to hurt.

Tears sprang to Melissa's eyes. She lowered her gaze, then raised it.

"Probably," she replied.

"Your truth would be much more interesting."

"How can you know that?"

"Because I do," I laughed. "Individual truth is the only interesting thing. If you found something deep in your heart to tell and told it well, that would be interesting."

"I believe that."

"But of course it would need to be compelling, and you would need to tell it well. That's the work."

"That would be the work."

"Nothing is interesting until a creator breathes some life and some beauty into it."

"The dancer book — it's been a crutch of some kind."

"Probably."

"Just telling my own story seems so much more arrogant."

"Yes."

"And personal. Too revealing, maybe."

"Yes."

"Do you think I could do such a thing?"

"I always presume that a person can."

She laughed. "And do they?"

"Some percentage of the time."

"A large percentage?"

"Some percentage."

She smiled and grew thoughtful.

"I do have a story I've wanted to tell," she resumed.

"Tell me about it."

"Tell me about it" is one of my favorite coaching phrases. Many beginning coaches fear hearing about the actual work, because they worry that they won't know what to do with the information. Are they supposed to gush and say, "Oh, that sounds so interesting!"? Are they supposed to critique and criticize: "Well, that won't do very well in the marketplace!"? Should they just listen and nod, presuming that the mere telling will prove helpful and even therapeutic? They are right to worry, because their task is even more sophisticated: it is to make instant judgments about whether or not their client's project sounds healthy.

These judgments might sound like the following: "I wonder if it's a good idea to write it from the point of view of the old woman when it's the girl's story? I can see why you might want to write in the old woman's voice, but won't that restrict what you can say about the girl? Isn't it a story that the girl has to tell? Or one that an omniscient narrator tells?" A creativity coach, just like a creator, attempts to hold the whole of the thing, the initiating impulse and the labyrinthine possibilities of the work as it is and as it might be, and from that awesome, intimate, and creative place wonder aloud and make suggestions.

In response to my "Tell me about it," Melissa replied, "A teenage girl comes home from school to find everything slightly off. A vase is on the wrong table. Some pictures have moved. First her mother doesn't come home from work, then her father doesn't come home. The main action of the — "

"Novel."

" — of the novel takes place in those hours while she's waiting for her folks to come home. She has fantasies, flashback memories of being abandoned, some surprising joy along with the dread — "

"What's happened to them?"

"I don't know."

"Because that isn't so important?"

"Right. What's important is her reaction to their having gone missing for a few hours."

"Write this novel."

Today, in the workshop I conducted, when we went around the room and participants announced what they were working on, Melissa didn't hesitate. "I'm working on a novel about a teenage girl whose parents go missing for a few hours and who enters a kind of dreamworld as she contemplates life without her parents." She didn't apologize for or denigrate her idea, she didn't, by word or gesture, act as if she needed permission from anyone to work on this novel. It was as if a serious soul had escaped from lockup. When, in the course of the workshop, it came time to write, Melissa wrote and wrote.

I'm back at the inn watching the rain fall on the Ohio River. Will Melissa write her novel? She certainly has a better chance now. If she can maintain that right self-relationship, if she can hire on her inner creativity coach, there's no doubt that she can write a draft of a novel. It might be a good draft, it might be a bad draft, but it would be written. If it were bad and if she didn't, out of disappointment and a stubborn refusal to take the next natural steps, fire her inner coach, she might revise it, revise it again, and make it true, beautiful, and good. If she were to become an effective self-coach, that could just maybe happen.

SKILL TWO

PASSIONATELY MAKING MEANING

The second skill I would like you to learn is so large that it is more a way of life than just a skill. I call it "passionately making meaning." This skill has five components. First, you need to decide how you will lead your life. This decision is the one you contemplated making in Exercise 2 from the last chapter: deciding to matter. Few people will support you in this decision, so you will have to fly in the face of others' opinions. Life is easier on cogs than on independent souls, gives more support to those who go along than to those who speak out. You, however, will be loud and independent. This is a *decision* you make.

You decide to matter, to live a principled, creative, active life in support of your cherished ideals, to manifest your potential, to do good work, in short, to make your life meaningful at least to you. You decide to make your life count for something. You do not presume that your life matters on a cosmic scale or that your efforts will move mountains. Rather, you embrace the idea of authenticity and proclaim your intention to live authentically.

Second, once you decide that you intend to matter, you announce the following: "Regardless of whether or not the universe is meaningful, of whether my odds of succeeding are long or short, of everything at both the existential level and at the practical level, I am going to intentionally make meaning." You decide to matter, and then you announce that you intend to make meaning. What you are saying is "there is no meaning until I make it." What you mean is "I am not going to sit around waiting for the universe, some guru, some book, some god, some workshop, or anything else to let me in on the secrets of the universe or the shape of my personal path. I am going to *decide,* based on my best understanding of reality and my life purposes, how I intend to make my meaning."

Third, you ask yourself the question, "What exactly are my life purposes? If I'm going to actively make meaning in accordance with my life purposes, I had better know them, articulate them, memorize them, and make sure that I really believe in them. So what are they?" That is, you need to identify your real reasons for living and the role or roles you intend to play in life. Your life purposes may be to fight against injustice, to live a better life, to make beautiful things, to do good deeds, and so on. These are the sorts of life purposes that are rich enough and big enough to count.

Coming up with one life purpose will probably not be enough. Take "battling injustice." Can you base a life on that purpose alone? I think not, even as profound a life purpose as that is. It turns out that a person who feels really alive has several life purposes in mind. These multiple life purposes fit together seamlessly into a composite and typically include the following six elements:

- making use of your innate talents and abilities, your heart, mind, and hands
- using your whole being every day, rather than intermittently or sporadically
- serving truth-telling and other important values
- getting genuine satisfaction out of life
- working hard on meaningful projects
- entering into loving relationships

These combine into a sentence that can become a person's life purpose statement: "I will make use of myself every day in the service of truth-telling and other important values while at the same time getting some real satisfaction out of life through love and work." This is a solid life purpose statement upon which a good life can be built.

However, it may not be yours. Try your hand at arriving at your own life purpose statement.

EXERCISE 3
Arriving at Your Life Purpose Statement

Spend the next few minutes naming your own life purposes. Remember that you can't know what actions to take until you know what deep purposes those actions are meant to serve. Ideally, everything you do in life, every change you contemplate, every decision you make, every action you take, connects to and flows from your life purposes. Try to articulate them now.

List your life purposes. Then, if you can, order and rank them. Are some purposes primary and others secondary? Do several combine into a single purpose? Take all the time you need as you work on this, since no other exercise is more important than this one. Once you have your life purposes named and ranked, create a single sentence of the sort I constructed above, a sentence that will become your instructions for living.

Now comes the fourth step. You need to hold the intention to fulfill your life purpose. That is, you need to keep your meaning-making efforts firmly in mind.

EXERCISE 4

Holding the Intention to Fulfill
Your Life Purposes

How will you hold the intention to live exactly as you intend? How will you remain mindful? When life resumes its habitual busyness, what will help you remember your intentions? Begin by finding a smooth stone or other small object that fits neatly into the palm of your hand. Close your fist around it and feel it. Squeeze it and repeat the life purpose statement that you constructed in the previous exercise. Squeeze it a second time and repeat your life purpose statement again. Do this as many times as you're willing to.

Hold your stone all day. Whenever you become aware of the stone in your clenched fist, repeat your life purpose statement. Much of the day you will forget that you are holding the stone. Just outside your conscious awareness, however, you won't have forgotten — either the stone or your life purpose statement. The longer you manage to hold the stone, the more firmly you will imprint your life purpose statement.

Sometimes your hand will get tired, and you will have to open it. Whenever that happens, repeat your life purpose statement. This will remind you that it is vital to remember your life purposes when you are tired, bothered, distracted, upset, and otherwise not in your best frame of mind.

Sleep with the stone under your pillow.

Hold it again tomorrow.

The ultimate goal, of course, is to hold the intention without having to hold the stone. However, you may want to keep the stone in your pocket for those times when you need an instant refresher course.

For your fifth step, you need to tackle this project with passion and energy. Remember that I am calling this skill "*passionately* making meaning." Perhaps you think it goes without saying that a person would naturally be passionate about something as central and vital to her life as her own life purposes. However, we know this isn't true. Few people live their lives passionately. Most people go through the motions, burdened by their tasks, their everyday work, their responsibilities, their own personalities. They live closer to depression than ecstasy, often in a perpetual crisis. Indeed, most people need convincing that it makes sense to be passionate about anything.

Why take the risks that opting for passion requires? People are trained to avoid displays of passion and even *feeling* passionate. They settle for a life that fails to nourish them, one that feels safe rather than wild and out-sized. Although they've probably never thought it through, they suspect that passion demands heroism — and they don't feel heroic. They fear that passion and madness are close friends. Yes, Beethoven was passionate — and look at how manic and disturbed a life he led. Yes, van Gogh was passionate — and he declined into a depression that ended in suicide. The average person looks at the headstrong, egocentric, heroic, mad passion of such artists and thinks, "Yikes! That's not for me!"

But it must be for you — although perhaps in a less dramatic form! Accepting the need to be passionate and finding ways to increase your passion are such important subjects that we will return to them in later chapters. Passion is the driving force that motivates us and fuels our meaning-making journey. Without it, we are exactly like a car without gas.

Let me repeat the five steps I've discussed in this lesson:

1. You decide to matter.

2. You accept that you must make meaning.

3. You identify your life purposes and articulate a life purpose statement.

4. You hold the intention to fulfill your life purposes.

5. You passionately act to fulfill your life purposes.

These five ideas comprise the skill of passionately making meaning. You rid yourself of depression, the feeling that life isn't worth living, and other existential ailments by adopting a way of life that is meaningful to you and by throwing yourself into projects that flow from your decisions about where you want to invest meaning. You successfully handle the obstacles to passionate meaning-making, many of which are profound, and the risks associated with passionate meaning-making, which are likewise numerous and real. In the process you learn how to spend your days in love with life.

I know this is a lot to learn in one lesson! However, I hope that you agree that these five steps form a seamless whole that can easily be taken together. They constitute a high path, one both creative and righteous. A person traveling this high path tries to make meaning consistent with her ideals and her best understanding of her life's purpose. The life she adopts, whether it is laying bricks, baking bread, or writing symphonies, must reflect her sense of how her values can be translated into the life she lives.

Translating our values into how we live is our main activity. Values guide us; the meaning we make sustains us. And because we recognize that meaning must be made and maintained, not sought after or found, we accept responsibility for restoring meaning when we lose it. The following story illustrates how one screenwriter worked to restore meaning in the context of Hollywood.

Los Angeles, California

I am invited to Los Angeles to speak about the creative process to two hundred Christian screenwriters, an interesting gig for an atheist who was born a Jew. Since I'll be in town, I contact my Los Angeles clients with whom I work by phone or email and see who wants to meet. It therefore happens that on a beautiful Tuesday afternoon in May I'm meeting with an Academy Award–winning screenwriter who is feeling miserable.

Previously I'd learned about her experience with that award-winning film. When all was said and done, exactly one line in the film remained that had any significance for her. Everything else had been diluted, changed, cut, censored, made friendlier, made more middle-America, made prettier, made more ordinary. She had intended the movie to be about insincere piety and the horrors of worship. Instead it became a love story, an adventure movie, and a suspense thriller, beautifully done in the Hollywood manner. It had gorgeous production values, a hypnotic score, superb acting. She hated it.

That experience made her want to write stage plays or to direct independent movies. But the money dangled before her eyes to doctor Hollywood scripts and to write new Hollywood scripts turned out to be irresistible. She was even given her own movie to write and direct, a great coup, although the movie that she managed to make was infinitely fluffier than the movie she had intended to make. Still, she could say that she was a Hollywood director. She was living high on the hog, an experience she found surreal, irritating, and altogether depressing.

She told me about the script that she really wanted to write, which was currently about a quarter finished. It was based on the true story of a band of Danish boys who were recruited as messengers by the Danish Resistance during

World War II. These boys bicycled, skied, ran, and walked messages among Resistance cells and between the Resistance and Allied spies in Denmark. She wanted to use that basic setup but had moved the action to France because she wanted a Catholic backstory and because she had a passionate desire to make a movie set in France.

Her movie would focus on one fourteen-year-old boy, Michael, the hero of the tale, who is given a vital message that he must get from Occupied France to Free France. There would be a love story, adventure, suspense, betrayals, and everything you would expect from a movie in this genre, except that she was also going to indict the Catholic Church for its wartime complicity and, worse, she was going to end fully on a down note. All the boys, our hero included, are tortured and killed by the Nazis. The message that Michael must deliver would get through to the Allies — the audience would get that satisfaction — but they would not get a Hollywood ending.

"A Hollywood movie would end with the message delivered and maybe the boy killed, but beautifully killed, sentimentally killed," she told me. "We would have some nice joy and some nice pathos. Not in my movie! In my movie the message gets delivered, but the movie continues for a full five minutes. Michael is tortured and fails. He gives up the names of all the other boys. We see them tortured and killed in turn. Nor is the torture some pretty little cattle prod thing that, because we're familiar with it from a thousand other movies, fails to affect us. In my movie we meet the 'Sardine Can Monster.' He was a real torturer who rolled down the skin on the backs of his victims like you open the lid of a sardine can." She paused. "I want people to throw up."

It was a script that needed major financing, which meant either that she would have to get several European studios to back it, a task that felt beyond her ability, or else she would have to feed it to the Hollywood machine, which she knew would squeeze the guts and truth out of it. She didn't want a pretty little Holocaust movie. She was convinced that she could never get it made as she envisioned it, and that conviction had completely stalled her. She wasn't writing, she wasn't moving ahead on other things, she was, in fact, paralyzed and depressed.

"Michael in the movie," I said. "He is living intensely."

"Yes."

"On a mission."

"Yes."

"The world is depending on him. Literally."

"Yes. Or close enough."

"Which is how you want to live."

"Of course! But I don't have a message to deliver through enemy lines — "

"Don't you?"

She stared at me. "How weird!" she exclaimed. "Of course that's true. I do believe that my movie could help save the world, not literally, but not figuratively either. It could have a real impact. And it does need to be delivered through enemy lines! I am on a mission!" She paused. "Or rather, I ought to be." After a moment she said, "I should go the European route. I'm teaching a workshop on screenwriting in Spain next month. Lots of European studio types are taking my workshop."

"What are you feeling?"

"It's too daunting! I'd rather be Michael. I'd rather be hiding in a forest, starving and wounded, than trying to sell my movie. That is such a crazy thing to say. But that's how I feel."

"He has a pure path to follow, pure in a dramatic sense. You have calls to make, email to send, rhetoric to frame. Michael is on an adventure, horrible as it is. You are a saleswoman. Michael is a swashbuckler. You sell used cars and deodorant. Your task is not so much arduous as it is boring. It is a matter of selling, selling, selling."

"Selling something that I'm convinced no one will buy."

"Yes."

"That's so draining and dispiriting."

"Yes."

"I would rather be Michael."

"Think about that. Let's meet again tomorrow. All right?"

That afternoon I go off to speak to the Christians. The conference, it turns out, is about marketing and not creativity, my address notwithstanding. The group is helped to see how their message must be embedded in a script that meets Hollywood where it's at. The keynote speaker, a wildly successful filmmaker who has made his mark producing short animated films whose gospel messages are presented by fruits and vegetables (I am serious), lectures the group on the necessity of understanding the needs, desires, and psychology of audiences. Do not preach, he tells them. Do not bore. Do not condescend. Embed your message in a narrative that works. Less message, more narrative action. Less message, more love story. Less message, more Hollywood. If you would sleep with lions...

Lunch, although boxed, is quite good. The Christians are friendly. Like any group of would-be scriptwriters, they are shaking their heads. "I want to get my message across, not hide it so perfectly in a Hollywood story that no one can find it!" They could be environmentalists, atheists, Buddhists, any group learning the strict lessons of mass communication, mass taste, the mass mind. They spear their melon balls and pineapple chunks and wail the same lament as my client's: "I want to do good work!" Their literal lament is "I want to do God's work!" but it amounts to the same sentiment.

The next day I meet my client in Westwood, since she has a meeting to attend on the UCLA campus after our session. "I want to live like Michael," she says. "Not as he lives, but with the feeling he has in his heart as he crosses France to deliver his message. I want to feel on a mission, even if all I'm doing is revising my script or setting up meetings with executives. I want to feel on a mission and not like I'm completely defeated by this system."

"Are you willing to lay down your life to tell this story?"

"As if having some meetings with European studio execs is 'laying down my life'!" she exclaims. "It brings up such feelings of self-loathing and cowardice. Why can't I make the effort to get my movie made, given that I have the connections, the credentials, the vision, the talent, the energy — every damn thing! Some scriptwriter off the street might have a ten-thousand-to-one chance of pulling this off. But my odds can't be much worse than a few hundred to one. And who cares about odds? What do odds mean to Michael? He must get his message delivered. I must get my message across. To hell with the odds!"

"So you're on a mission?"

"I am, damn it!"

Because she would be in Europe for much of the time, the next month we correspond by email. I learn that a famous European director fell head over heels in love with her script idea but nevertheless passed on the project. A Hollywood director begs to see the quarter-script, loves it, then gets cold feet. Producers pass. Directors pass. Actors pass. Over the coming months I hear about this no, that maybe, this almost-yes. We work on other things. Does she retain her sense that she is on a mission through these long months? Only fleetingly.

"I'm no closer to getting this made," she says at one point. "Actually, I'm much further away. I've been in contact with everyone I know, and they've all passed."

"And?"

"And I still think of Michael. Maybe it'll take five years. Maybe it'll take ten years. Maybe it'll never happen. I'll live my life and do other things. I can't maintain this life-and-death mission feeling day in and day out. It can't be done and doesn't even make sense. I need other things out of life. I'm not actually on the run from Nazis. I can

soak in the sun, walk by the ocean, find some love. But I'm
not about to forget Michael. I'm not forgetting my commitment. Do you believe me?"

She signs on to doctor the script of a hundred-million
dollar project. Then she gets a Hollywood movie to direct.
Sometimes I get an email: "I haven't given up on Michael!"
Had she? No, Michael was still in her heart. She still made
the occasional effort to find support for her project. But
was she passionate about the project day in and day out? Was
she fervent? Was she still on a mission? No. The movie
was simply too unwanted. No amount of fervor could
counteract that terrible fact.

To this day, there is no happy ending. If I were making
a Hollywood movie, I'd have to contrive one. Some exec-
utive would be on my back, nagging, cajoling, threatening
to pull the plug on the picture. "You can't end it there!
Give them something, for God's sake!" What can I give
you? That, all things considered, and despite the lack of
prospects for her worthy movie, my client could feel
justifiably proud of her meaning-making efforts? Yes, I can
give you that at least.

SKILL THREE

GETTING A GRIP ON YOUR MIND

The Buddha said, "Get a grip on your mind!" There is no more important lesson to learn. Wrong thinking, which we ourselves create and perpetuate, causes us needless suffering and prevents us from creating deeply, meeting the art marketplace, and living well. This wrong thinking comes in many forms. It appears as self-battering and self-bashing. It comes disguised as "objective thinking" designed to mask our anxieties, doubts, and fears. It comes as bravado, stubbornness, and rage. Wrong thinking is a surrender and a defeat and a creativity self-coach's prime enemy.

If you are going to act as a self-coach, you need to become your own cognitive therapist. You need to take an active interest in how you think, what you think, why you think what you think, and how you can change your thoughts and thought patterns. This is intricate work because you need to become aware of many subtleties. The thoughts that hamper and hinder us can sound so innocent! And the reason they sound so innocent is that we ourselves have made them that way so that we won't notice what's really going on. In fact, you will have to expose your own tricks to yourself. It will be very brave of you to do this — and you must!

Start with the following exercise, which will give you a sense of the subtleties involved.

EXERCISE 5
Noticing Anxious Self-Talk

We often choose to say things to ourselves in a way that allows us to mask the anxiety we are feeling. Following are eleven characteristic linguistic tricks we use to cover up our anxiety. Look over the list and see if any of these statements look familiar to you. Then think through — and write about — how you might handle anxiety without relying on these linguistic ruses.

1. *"I'm not ready."*
   "I'm not quite ready to get started on this canvas."
   "I don't think I'll be ready to play my new repertoire for at least another month."

2. *"I don't feel like it."*
   "I just don't feel like showing him my work."
   "I don't feel like auditioning for parts that require an accent."

3. *"I don't feel well."*
   "I never feel very well right before choral rehearsal."
   "I don't feel well enough to meet those collectors tonight."

4. *"I can't think straight."*
   "I just can't think straight about this term paper."
   "I always feel spaced out in critique sessions."

5. *"I can't do it."*
   "I couldn't ask such a famous artist to look at my work."
   "I can't play my instrument well on muggy days."

6. *"I don't know what to say."*
   "I never know what to say when people tell me they like my work."
   "I have this screenplay I want to write but I don't know how to begin it."

7. *"I can't see the point."*
   "I can't see the point in auditioning for that — I'm just not the type."
   "I can't see the point in approaching a gallery owner cold."

8. *"It feels too difficult."*
"It feels too hard working with watercolors."
"I could make a short video, but a long one feels too hard."

9. *"What's happening here?"*
"Oh, I had no idea there'd be critiquing in this class!"
"Nowhere in the class description did it say we'd be performing in front of an audience!"

10. *"I do better with..."*
"I'd do better with a collaborator who knew how to score a film."
"I'd do better working on smaller canvases."

11. *"Yes, but..."*
"Yes, I should get my paper ready, but there's a whole two days left."
"Yes, I should enter that piano competition, but I don't really have a chance."

Just *really* noticing what you say to yourself can make a world of difference. Aaron Beck, one of the founders of cognitive therapy, explained:

A patient reported that he felt blue every time he made a mistake and he couldn't understand why he should feel this way. He fully accepted the notion that there was nothing wrong in making mistakes and that it was an inevitable part of living. He was instructed to focus on his thoughts the next time he felt an unpleasant affect in connection with making a mistake. At the next interview he reported the observation that whenever he made a mistake he would think "I'm a dope" or "I never do anything right" or "How can anybody be so dumb?" After having one of these thoughts he would become depressed. By becoming aware of these self-criticisms, however, he was able to recognize how unreasonable they were. This recognition seemed to remove the sting from his blue reactions. (*Cognitive Therapy of Depression* [New York: Guilford, 1987])

Psychology professor Robert Boice, who does cognitive work with blocked writers, had them first notice their wrong thinking and then substitute more helpful thoughts:

Initially, the cognitions of these blocked writers were typically counterproductive to writing. Clients at this stage tended to list thoughts that encouraged avoidance (e.g., "I really have to get the car washed"), that demeaned the task (e.g., "Most of what gets published today is garbage; why should I add to it?"), or that simply distracted them (e.g., "I wonder what I'll make for dinner tomorrow?"). Emphasis in early therapy sessions was placed on recognizing how these thoughts interfered with writing by competing for time and/or by inducing anxiety and self-doubt. Later, attention was shifted toward thought substitution. Clients were taught, via modeling and other tactics, to substitute more positive and relaxing thoughts that would help them get on task. (*Professors as Writers* [Stillwater, Okla.: New Forums Press, 1990])

You can use the following simple three-step procedure when you act as your own cognitive therapist: First, you notice your thoughts and identify those that don't serve you. This means growing aware of your linguistic tricks and understanding what your self-talk actually signifies. Second, you dispute those self-sabotaging thoughts. You say — silently or out loud — "No, I don't buy that!" Third, you substitute a new, useful thought.

Here is how this process would sound:

Example One

"I can't write if I outline. Outlining kills the creative spark in me."

"No! It's just that I'm feeling anxious about outlining my article and want an excuse to run from the task."

"I can write with an outline, and I can write without an outline. I can even write in the shower with a bar of soap! I can do whatever is necessary, and today what seems necessary is that I quiet my nerves, sit still, and outline."

Example Two

"For some people, writing is easy. For me, it is very hard. Therefore, I must not be a writer."

"Wow, was that a wonderful excuse!"

"Sometimes writing is easy, and sometimes writing is hard. So sometimes I will have it easy, and sometimes I will have it hard. Welcome to life."

Example Three

"I can't possibly write before breakfast. My rumbling stomach would distract me."

"Right! Very cute, mind."

"I can write morning, noon, and night."

You can train yourself to have these simple but important conversations with yourself. You can learn to talk yourself out of not creating, not meeting the marketplace, not risking, not living. But you must *train* yourself, because the significance of your self-statements may not be obvious to you until you are practiced at understanding your tricks. "I'm hungry" may mean "I can't think of what to paint next." "I'm so upset with my husband!" may mean "I am so upset with the choice I made to become a graphic designer!" "I have no time for anything creative" may mean "I can't see the point of trying to paint when I can't even draw." Our self-statements are often dodges, games, excuses, and defensive maneuvers, and it takes practice and courage to see them for what they are.

Most of our thoughts have either an obvious or a hidden self-referential component. That is, most of them are, at least in part, about us. Our brain rumbles along, monitoring information submitted by our senses, following trains of thought that caught its attention decades ago or just yesterday, and popping into our conscious awareness our current thoughts, almost all of which are ultimately about us. This phenomenal process presents us with countless thoughts that must be monitored, thoughts that can't be taken at face value.

A thought like "She looks good in red" may mean "I am so fat and such a loser!" We can spiral into a depression just by having the innocent-sounding "She looks good in red" pop into our conscious awareness. If we let that thought go by without understanding that it is really a charge we are making against ourselves, we risk injuring ourselves and ruining our chances of creating for that day. We want to stop self-injurious thoughts from attacking us by *instantly* comprehending their meaning and by actively disputing them.

Paul Salmon and Robert Meyer taught a cognitive-behavioral approach to the treatment of performance anxiety. They described one of their clients: "Diane, an organist, was terrified of playing her music from memory. Doing so made her so anxious that she avoided it whenever possible. 'I have a poor memory,' is the way she first described the problem. To cope with this problem, she learned to monitor her 'stream of consciousness' for self-defeating thoughts that tended to discourage and distract her. She also employed a technique called 'thought stopping,' in which she consciously terminated such thoughts *as soon as* she became aware of them" (*Notes from the Green Room* [San Francisco: Jossey-Bass, 1998]). By consciously disputing self-injurious thoughts *as soon as you think them,* you stop them in their tracks.

The third step, after identifying and disputing wrong thinking, is replacing the wrong thought with a right one. The simplest way of doing this is to prepare in advance a few all-purpose affirmations and to use one of them as a thought substitute when a negative thought intrudes. This is what you will do in your next exercise.

EXERCISE 6
Using Affirmations as Thought Substitutes

An affirmation is a short, simple, positive, declarative phrase that you say to yourself because you want to think a certain way (more confidently, more optimistically) or because you want to aim yourself in a certain direction (toward your artwork, toward marketing your artwork). Affirmations can serve as substitutes for our characteristically negative self-talk. The following are some simple, all-purpose affirmations:

- I am fine just as I am.
- I am off to create.
- I trust my resources.

- I am not worried.

- I am perfectly okay.

- I can handle this.

- First things first.

- I accept myself.

- I am capable and courageous.

- I have everything I need.

- One step at a time.

- I am ready.

Please create a few affirmations of your own, just two or three, that you can memorize and have available when a self-defeating thought intrudes. Test your affirmations out on your next negative thought and check to see if they are robust enough to do the job. If they aren't, go back to the drawing board and try again.

It is brilliant work to identify your wrong thinking, dispute it, and provide yourself with thought substitutes. Even better is growing aware of the causes of your wrong thinking. It is one thing to recognize that when you say, "I am too tired to paint" you actually mean, "I can't think of any reasons to paint." It is even better to get to the root causes of your negative thinking and change your mind at a deeper level. If, for instance, you suddenly had good reasons to paint, no longer feared making mistakes and messes, stopped doubting your abilities and your chances, and in other ways large and small were "thinking right" about painting, negative thoughts would only rarely arise. You would only need to use the "treatment" occasionally — you would be virtually cured.

The goal, then, is to acquire the right mind-set, out of which right thinking flows. This desired mind-set has many components. You must cherish truth, beauty, and goodness, brush away mistakes and failures, turn first to your own wisdom in all matters, frown at idleness, revere work, and so on. You must honor perseverance and the realities of the creative process, ignore criticism, come back from rejection — there is so much! However, it is all known to you if you quietly listen to the truth that you already possess.

"Getting a grip on your mind" means two complementary but different things: eliminating wrong thinking and championing right thinking. As a creativity self-coach, your job description includes both these magnificent tasks.

Savannah, Georgia

I have come to Savannah, in the heat and humidity of July, to do a series of workshops at the Savannah College of Art and Design, billed as the "largest art school in the world." SCAD is a phenomenon, a recent addition to the world of art schools and a big player in the rejuvenation of Savannah. SCAD's method is to purchase fanciful and fantastic

run-down or abandoned buildings throughout town, reno-
vate them (they have an award-winning renovation major),
and add them to the fold. The library is a former downtown
department store; you can attend classes in an old fire sta-
tion or a Masonic lodge.

My wife and I are put up at Casey House, the college's
upscale period guesthouse, and treated royally. The experience is nevertheless disturbing for folks like us who have
never been to the South before. To our eyes, slavery has
ended in name only. The gulf between the races is so huge
that it taints everything. I find myself inadvertently hum-
ming the theme to *Gone with the Wind* as we wander
Savannah's famous squares and haunted sights.

I am working with various constituencies at SCAD
during my weeklong stay: the counseling staff, who deliver
mental health services to the school's students; the resi-
dence directors and assistants, who mind the students in
the dorms; the graduate students, who will have to face the
real world before too long; and the faculty. My work with
faculty consists of a two-hour chat. I wonder if anyone will
attend. Only a portion of the faculty is around during the
summer, it is a blistering Friday afternoon, and, if they are
like me, they must certainly prefer drinking something
with ice in it than coming to the student center to hear a
lecture. To my amazement, fifty faculty members show up.

At the end of the lecture I chat and sign books and
notice that one faculty member is hanging back, waiting
for his chance at a private talk.

"I don't teach here," he informs me. "I teach mathematics

at the University of Georgia. I made the trip to Savannah because I wanted to talk to you for a few minutes, because of something you wrote in one of your books about self-forgiveness. Can I get ten minutes of your time?"

We find a corner table. There he formally introduces himself with his name and rank of full professor.

"It's actually hard to say what's on my mind," Martin begins.

"You mean that it's painful to say, or that you don't know what you want to say?"

"Both," he replies. "The painful part is that the universe has played me for a fool. As to the other, I don't know how to proceed."

"Tell me about the painful part."

He looks up. "My mathematical specialty is Elgar Transformational Equations. They are terrifically elegant theoretical equations that were presumed to connect to string theory and that, if only one could penetrate them, would become the tool by which new discoveries in math and physics would happen. I began studying them twenty years ago as a postdoc, when their beauty seduced me. But in the last three or four years they've turned out to be chimeras. No, it's more like five years already. Five years! They've turned out to be false — even though some of my colleagues hold out the possibility that with some tweaking they'll still prove solid and valuable. But all the young mathematicians have moved on to Tanaka Transformational Equations, which look to be more robust and, well, flat-out correct. As opposed to ours, which look to be just wrong."

It would have surprised Martin to learn that I had started out in life hoping to become an astronomer, that I went to a high-powered math and science high school, and that I was invested in science enough to spend the summer between my junior and senior years taking a class in vector calculus at the Hayden Planetarium. So as it happens, as someone who, when given a book report assignment in the fourth grade, chose to do it on Newton's *Mathematica Principia*, I have some special empathy for Martin's predicament.

"Yours were elegant but wrong. That doesn't seem fair."

"A cosmic joke," Martin replies sadly.

"And you feel like a fool?"

"A bloody idiot."

"And your reputation — "

"Don't have one."

"And to switch horses in midstream — "

"Can't! Too much math to learn. Terribly hard transformational equations, intricate, mind-breaking. I barely understand the math of my own theory! To switch would be like trying to learn Chinese when you've spent a lifetime on Icelandic."

"Are there any guarantees that these other transformational equations are correct?"

"No! Because all string theory is in doubt! I could learn Chinese and discover that I really needed to learn Italian! Maybe — " He hesitated. "It's ridiculous to give odds, but I think there's a fifty-fifty chance that the Tanaka Equations will work. Maybe even slightly better odds than that."

"So what you're saying is that with a better guarantee you would try to learn them?"

"I don't know," Martin replies glumly.

"But you could master them, if you wanted to?"

"I don't know."

"Let me see if I follow. Math is where you decided to make meaning. You loved it and invested all your intellectual capital in it. Not only that, but you made a specific choice and opted to make the Elgar Equations your life's work, because they were beautiful, because you had an intuition that they were the genuine article, because you had high hopes for them. You invested in what looked to be a champion thoroughbred, and you lost. Now you must make new meaning."

"There's nothing else. I'm a broken man."

"Tell me, these other equations, the Tanaka Equations, do they interest you?"

"Interest me? I'm not sure what you mean."

"Can you see loving them? Studying them? Going to bed with them? Savoring them? Or — this is also possible — are you tired of math?"

Martin thinks.

"They don't interest me. I don't think any transformational equations interest me anymore. I think I hate math."

I wait for Martin to assimilate this important news.

"But that's what I do. I teach mathematics. That's how I use my brain. If I didn't — "

"Since you have tenure, you could begin cheating your students. Who could complain? You could mail in your lessons."

"Excuse me?"

"If it occurred to you that you had to find something new to love, but you also wanted to continue teaching math because that was your livelihood, then you might be inclined to start delivering half-hearted lectures on the material or, worse, you might start canceling classes, or, I don't know, you might start drinking whiskey in the morning. So there's that to consider."

Martin was listening closely. "Let me see if I'm following you. I should find a new intellectual love and also find a way to teach math honorably, if I continue to teach it."

"Exactly."

"I've invested meaning in Elgar Transformational Equations for twenty-five years!" Martin exclaims. "Twenty-five years!"

"That's a very brave thing to say, the way you just said it. And now you need to get a grip on your mind."

"I feel terrible," Martin whispers. "Just terrible."

"It was a personal tragedy to have picked the wrong horse, to have chosen a beautiful horse that couldn't win the race. Now you must dismount, sit on the ground, cry some bitter tears, and then stand up and find a new love."

Martin does look ready to cry.

"There's a Sufi saying," I continue. "From Saadi of Shariz. It goes like this: 'I fear that you will not reach Mecca, O Nomad! For the road which you are following leads to Turkestan!' You were on one road, and you must get off it now. You must find a new intellectual love. You simply must." I pause. "What do you really love?"

"I love Bach."

"Yes."

"I would love to play the *Well-Tempered Clavier* really well."

"That's a nice challenge. But it's not a life's work. That isn't quite it."

Martin thinks. "I'd like to understand what's known about evolution and figure out where I stand. I have a rough sense of the controversies, a rough sense of what punctuated equilibrium means and why it's the leading explanatory candidate. I can also sense why it isn't satisfying and why the arguments from design are so potent, even if they are championed by creationists. Maybe every evolutionary paleontologist knows something that I don't know, and maybe I could get my questions answered in an hour. Or maybe they don't know the secret — maybe that is superfertile ground for a person to investigate with a true beginner's mind."

"That is an intellectual challenge!" I agree. "What do you think?"

"I'm forty-eight years old. Scientists make their great discoveries when they're young."

"That's just wrong thinking. Get a grip on your mind. Say something different."

"I'm still young. And some scientists have done important work in their fifties."

"Better. Try again."

"I'm young and I have interesting work ahead of me."

"Excellent! Write that down."

He pulls out his pad and does just that.

"Here's my next piece of wrong thinking. I'm a mathematician. I can't fool around in other scientists' fields. That's their province."

"Fine. Now, what's right thinking?"

"Who gives a shit about those categories! There was a time when every thinking person was a natural scientist, he or she did philosophy, biology, physics, art, everything. To hell with categories, compartments, departments, and pigeonholes!"

"Excellent. You are cooking! What else will get in your way? What other forms of wrong thinking will stop you?"

"I can't think of them all. But I see their general nature, their general outline. Because I've been so angry and disappointed, I haven't been able to move forward. I've been completely stuck on feeling cheated. As if math were so much higher or more meaningful than other intellectual pursuits. I need one overarching mantra — maybe this is it."

"Yes?"

"I go where the thinking takes me."

"Nice!" I pause. "What if those new areas require a lot of investigation? What if — ?"

Martin interrupts me. "A lot is not the same as too much. I can hear the difference. The first is fine, the second is wrong thinking. I think my mantra there is 'Forests, not trees.' If I were doing theoretical physics I would need to deal with trees. But I have the feeling that I can do rich, interesting work in areas that interest me without needing to know tons of details. More like a smart science writer than a specialist scientist. I can picture how that would work."

"We are done," I say. "Yes?"

"Eric, I feel free of transformational equations."

"But you'll still have to honorably teach them."

"I understand."

"And it will still hurt your heart that you spent so many years riding that horse. But the pain will lessen as you move on."

"I can see that. I can spend forty years thinking about new things. I have tenure, a great life, astounding opportunities."

"In that case — "

"What do I owe you for this session?"

"Send me a souvenir from the University of Georgia."

It is on account of this brief creativity coaching session that my wife and I return from Savannah to find a pair of bulldog mugs awaiting us.

SKILL FOUR

ELIMINATING DUALISTIC THINKING

n the previous chapter we looked at how "wrong thinking" derails the creative impulse. The main kind of wrong thinking we examined was negative self-talk, statements that indict us, cause us to doubt, make us lose hope, and so on. I'm sure that you have at least a passing understanding of negative self-talk and probably have even tried to do something about it at one time or another. I'm also sure that the wrong thinking that we'll be looking at in this chapter will be rather more unfamiliar to you. It is *dualistic thinking*. In its own way, it is just as important to eradicate as negative thinking.

We possess powerful reasons for creating: it makes use of our potential, connects us to our long-held dreams, allows for an intellectually rich life, provides us with the satisfaction of accomplishment, and more. We also possess powerful reasons for *not* creating: it is real work; takes more of our mind, heart, and hands than we are accustomed to using; provokes anxiety; opens us up to the possibility of mistakes and messes; and so on. Most people let the negatives outweigh the positives and avoid creating. Many select creative projects that don't do their talent or spirit justice but that possess the apparent virtues of being easy and manageable. Only a few people opt for the creative life with *all* its positives and negatives. I'm sure that you hope to count yourself in this group.

When a person opts for the fully creative life, then she must do what is required of her to combat the powerful anticreating forces aligned against her. These forces arise from within her own being, from her culture, and just from being alive on this planet. One of the most important things that she must do is refuse to take sides with dualities like process and product, simplicity and complexity, discipline and flexibility, and so on, dualities that are integral parts of the creative process. Rather, she must accept *both* parts of each pair and come to a real understanding of the value of each, the place of each in the creative process. Then she can become a *holistic creator,* someone who has learned not to arbitrarily and defensively exclude options.

The moment I hear a client say that he favors process over product (or, more rarely, product over process) or that he favors simplicity over complexity (or, more rarely, complexity over simplicity), I suspect that he is in the habit of making excuses, that he doesn't fully understand the creative process, and that he must frequently be creatively blocked. Just as one goal of an aware Taoist is to identify the principles of yin and yang and to use their power to serve his ends so that in a given situation he manifests either more yin or more yang, the goal of a creative person is to honor *both* partners of every dualistic pair by choosing the quality that he will manifest at different times. If he refuses to do this honoring, he is not yet aboard the creative train.

When he does finally board that train, on some days he will say, "I am process oriented" and other days he will say, "I am product oriented." His focus is on his life mission and the needs of the project in front of him, not on abstract and perhaps even empty distinctions like "spiritual" versus "material" or "being" versus "doing." Indeed, these distinctions are often more illusory than real. Whether they are real or illusory, however, is irrelevant. What matters is that people often use these distinctions to excuse themselves from doing what they need to do. They use the language of abstract ideas to manage their anxiety and as a cover for avoiding their work.

People use the language of duality to avoid the creative imperative. They claim to "champion process" because they don't want to struggle or suffer a defeat. Rather than stick to the work in front of them, they announce that it's "their process" to take the month off. Or they claim to "champion simplicity" so as not to think hard, when hard thinking is exactly what's required of them. They explain that they'll wait until the matter becomes clearer. To continue with our Taoist analogy, it's as if they were choosing either yin or yang to champion, exclaiming when confronted by dirty dishes, "That's women's work" or apologizing when faced with a math problem, "Only men know math."

A human being does the dishes and does math. He or she doesn't use the ideas of masculine and feminine to avoid necessary action. Similarly, a creative person does everything she needs to do to create deeply. She doesn't use language to make excuses and justify her disinclination to create. As another way of getting a grip on her mind, she gets a grip on the way that language allows her to hide out. She bravely cries, "I will not use language that way!"

What dualistic pairs do would-be creators use to avoid creating? Here are a few of them: attachment and detachment, process and product, personal and commercial, work and play, idea and expression, discipline and flexibility, individuality and relationship, material and spiritual, being and doing, knowing and feeling, simplicity and complexity, mind and body. There are many, many more, because virtually any aspect of existence can be turned into a pair of (real or seemingly real) polar opposites. Sometimes we should be silent; sometimes we should speak; if we are not careful we can make one or the other into some kind of special virtue, simply because we want justification for keeping silent or for speaking up. We turn two aspects of existence into a duality and then call one nobler than the other to justify and excuse our behavior. As a creativity self-coach, you will learn to stop doing this.

Embracing Dualities

Make a long list of the dualities that seem inherent in the creative process. Start with the twelve pairs I listed above and add as many more pairs as come to mind. Allow your list to grow as long as it needs to grow. (Here are some more examples: fiction and nonfiction, art and craft, fine art and graphic art, rock and jazz, practice and performance, solitude and sociability.) Don't worry if your list grows very long, because there is nothing to fear.

Next, take each pair on your list, one at a time, and for each member of the pair say the following:

"Attachment is available to me. Detachment is available to me. Both principles are available to me, and I honor both equally."

and

"Process is available to me. Product is available to me. Both principles are available to me, and I honor both equally."

and

"Personal is available to me. Commercial is available to me. Both principles are available to me, and I honor both equally."

Think through what you are saying! When, for instance, you affirm that "personal" and "commercial" are both available to you as active principles, what you are saying is something like the following: "I understand that I have a real desire to do personal work, and I also understand that if I want to communicate that work to others and/or make a living from that work, I must acknowledge and deal with the marketplace. I have to make sense of both aspects of my existence, and I must avoid stubbornly championing the personal, as if only my desires counted, or the commercial, as if nothing mattered except worldly success. Sometimes I will champion the personal more, sometimes I will turn more of my attention to the marketplace. However I marry these two ideas, whatever compromises I choose to make or not make, whichever direction I go in, to whatever extent I keep my work private or endeavor to take it public, I will do so consciously, forthrightly, in accordance with my best understanding of my life's mission." Yes, that is a mouthful! But that is exactly the kind of chat you want to have with yourself as you affirm each element of these various pairs.

Continue all the way to the end of your list. When you finish, conclude with: "*Everything* is available to me."

A creative person who is in charge of his creative life acquires the habit of stepping back from these dualities so that he can ask himself, "To get on with my meaningful work, should I manifest discipline or flexibility at this moment?" This is very different from habitually saying, "I must be disciplined!" or, "I must be flexible!" To turn either member of a dualistic pair into an iron-clad principle is to make excuses and to avoid creating. As one painter put it, "Sometimes I start with an image. Sometimes I address the blank canvas. I prefer neither method." Holistic creating is rooted in the following principle: "I have no preferences. I do whatever is necessary and best."

EXERCISE 8

Eliminating Dualities

In the previous exercise you embraced both elements of various dualistic pairs. Now I would like you to practice eliminating dualities altogether.

You do this by breaking the habit of framing matters in terms of pairs and pairings. Instead of saying, "Should I be more disciplined or more spontaneous?" you say, "What does my work require of me?" Instead of saying, "Should I write fiction or nonfiction?" you say, "What shall I write?" Instead of saying, "Should I continue researching my book or should I begin writing it?" you say, "What does my book need today?" Instead of saying, "Should I work on my painting or get some textiles ready for the crafts fair?" you say, "What will I create today?"

This process brings about a profound change. You begin to make decisions based on an integrative, holistic, nondualistic basis rather than in accordance with the connotations that words like *research, craft,* and *discipline* carry. You gain freedom and clarity. You start each day fresh, you start each moment fresh, and you return to each project fresh. Be mindful today of the way that these insidious dualities creep into your mind and practice consciously eliminating them.

We make our own grief by choosing to align with one side or another of these dualities. We say, "I must do commercial work!" or, "I must do personal work!" and miss the possibility of doing integrative work that satisfies both masters. We say, "It's only good if it's simple!" or, "It's only worthy if it's complex!" and ignore the obvious truth that a single brushstroke carries the complexity of a human life and a complex idea can wow us with its elegant simplicity. When we let go of these distinctions — which are not necessarily false but can nevertheless lead us down the wrong path — and create as an apple tree produces apples, we stop fighting with ourselves, blocking ourselves, and creating work that is smaller than our deepest natural desires.

Holistic creating is the process of shedding excuses, dismissing fears, and transcending dualities. Not all pain and difficulty will vanish because you have learned how to create holistically. But learning to create in this way is a necessary component of a creativity self-coaching program. The mantra of this lesson therefore is: "I am whole, and I do what's necessary." As a final exercise, describe what "holistic creating" means to you. If you find that you can't, maybe the story that follows will clarify the picture. If you find that you can, congratulations!

Marin County, California

I was working with the bass player of a world-famous rock band that had broken up five years previously. At the moment Mark was hiding out in a bucolic corner of Marin County, that upscale San Francisco Bay Area enclave known, because of its wealth, beauty, and eccentric ways, as "Marvy Marin." Mark had parlayed his ecological, New Age, and Eastern interests into a life as an ostrich farmer, which, in Marin, is a perfectly normal pursuit.

He had a lot of money that his manager doled out to him. Mark had to make a case for all large expenditures and sometimes had to beg for money. He'd had to beg for the funds to buy his ostrich farm, since his manager had said, "An ostrich farm? Are you nuts?" His manager lived in Los Angeles, where fantasies take on different forms.

"Ian Anderson is a salmon farmer," Mark had replied.

"He probably knows something about what he's doing. What do you know? Plus, he stopped having hits! What was Jethro Tull's last hit? Plus, that's salmon! Everybody eats salmon! Who do you know who ever ate an ostrich?"

"I'll learn. And people eat ostrich. And ostrich eggs."

"Do music, for Christ's sake!"

"Have you ever had an ostrich egg omelet?"

"You want to buy a ranch because you had a good omelet?"

"I didn't actually have it. I saw Julia Child make one."

"Brilliant!"

In fact, it *was* brilliant. Mark longed to be around nature and animals and wanted to do something with his life that had nothing to do with music, touring, publicity, and, especially, other musicians. He wanted peace, and he could afford it. He wanted to stop smoking marijuana, which was a problem, and he wanted to be in love with a woman who loved him, which was an even bigger problem. He fancied that he had what the Buddhists called a greedy mind and believed himself too hungry for drugs, sex, songs, cities, fame, experiences — everything. None of that was him, he told me. He wanted to stop all that and find his way.

He'd remained adamant with his manager, gotten his money, bought a farm, stocked it with ostriches, and was now supplying fancy Bay Area restaurants with ostrich eggs and meat. He loved it. We had been working together for four years, since a year after the group broke up. Our first task was sobriety. We spent the first eighteen months on virtually nothing but not using marijuana. Then we spent a year on his relational life. He had never had a good relationship with a woman — he had always been the one dumped. That was almost unheard of for a rock star. Mark knew that there was something in his personality that made him choose women who didn't love him or even like him. We talked about that.

All this was wonderful work and had nothing to do with music. At the same time he was sad about the band breaking up and about no longer making music. His music and his creative life were subjects that were always nearby, waiting and needing to be addressed. Although we talked little about music, everything we were working on was preparation for his returning to a musical life.

Mark and I met monthly at my café-office. For some months running it became clear that the need to get back into music was growing in him. He was practicing again, both his bass playing and his singing. He was writing songs. He was going to clubs and concerts. He was reconnecting with the old crowd of musicians and meeting the young crowd. He began to grow enthusiastic about this or that guitar player, this or that band. All this was sporadic, but the signs were there that he meant to go public soon.

This brought up every manner of issue. The headline for what he was feeling was "I don't want to do it the way I did it before." We talked about what "before" had been like and what he hoped would be different this time around. This time he wanted his own songs played, he wanted to front the band, he wanted real control, he wanted to be the boss. At the same time, none of that sat well with him. He couldn't really picture himself as the star of a rock band, and he wasn't sure that he wanted to live that hard and fast. One minute he wanted it, the next minute he didn't. We tangoed for several sessions, then met on a beautiful afternoon in November for what turned out to be a pivotal session.

"I want to start the band."

"All right."

"No, I mean it. I want my own band. I want to be out front."

"Great! And?"

"I don't think I can do it."

"You can write songs."

"Yes."

"You can sing."

"Yes."

"You can hold an audience."

"Yes."

"But you can't be the lead singer of your own band?"

"No."

"Because?"

"I'm scared shitless? Is that what we seem to be saying?"

"Is it?"

"No."

"So?"

"Because I once wet my bed at summer camp — "

"Be serious."

"I don't know why!"

"How are you framing it to yourself?"

"As a personality issue. I think I'm telling myself, you don't have the rock star personality, the rock star mentality."

"Maybe it isn't precisely a personality issue. It may be that, without realizing it, you've chosen one life principle over another. You understand yin and yang?"

"Yes."

"That rock-and-roll life, what was it?"

"Yang!"

"Which do you prefer, yin or yang?"

He thought for a minute.

"Yin," he said. He thought about it. "Is that it?"

"What does yin represent?"

"Process. Submission. Being gentle. Taking a back seat. Getting out of the way. Being a servant. Helping."

"Does that sound like the lead singer of a rock-and-roll band?"

"It does not!"

"What does yang represent?"

"Domination. Power. Leading. Drive. Not giving a shit. And — this is so weird — heaven."

"Which do the Chinese say guides creation?"

"Yang."

"The sun, heat, light?"

"Yang."

"Who in the band was most concerned that every song ended perfectly, that each song had that sense of completeness to it?"

"Me."

"What is completion?"

"A yin thing."

"What is a concern with material forms — like ostrich eggs?"

"A yin thing."

"Name a yang drug."

"Speed."

"Name a yin drug."

"Marijuana."

"What was your drug of choice?"

"Marijuana."

"Who discards women?"

"Yang."

"Who is discarded?"

"Yin."

"You thought that you had a greedy mind. What is a greedy mind?"

"Yang."

"Was that ever you?"

"No. I impersonated yang."

I waited.

"So what does this mean?" he said.

"That, for whatever reason — constitutional, familial, archetypal, hormonal, cosmological — you favor a yin way of being. Yang energy makes you uncomfortable. Yang thinking makes you uncomfortable. You can see yourself off to the side of the stage, playing, but you can't see yourself dead center, the focus of all the attention, the leader, the boss. You can see yourself as a yin musician but not as a yang one. But, as a yin musician, you give up control. You submit. You know that you don't want to do that again. You're happy to cooperate but not to submit. To get to that place of cooperation, you need to step into yang, into leadership, power, dominance. Then you can step back and let your yin nature create harmony. But the starting place — "

"Is yang."

"Is yang. You've let your natural favoritism for yin

become a guiding principle. It holds sway. Now you need to make a conscious decision to uphold yang as well. After some time of doing that, maybe after a year or two of doing that, yin and yang will vanish as opposing principles, and you'll possess them both as complements of each other. You'll lead when it's right to lead and follow when it's right to follow. You'll be versatile and complete."

He sighed. "Where do I start?"

"Who hired new band members? You had three or four drummers during the band's life, right?"

"Four drummers. Alex picked them." Alex was the lead singer, the star, the driving force of the band.

"Choosing band members is — ?"

"Yang! I washed my hands of that process. Then I bitched about Alex's choices."

"If you want your own band, what do you need to do?"

"Among many other things, pick band members."

"How does that feel?"

"Damned yang!"

"Because?"

Mark thought. "Because the temptation is to be agreeable. The temptation is to submit. The temptation is to choose the first guitar player and the first drummer I encounter, so as not to have to say no to anybody."

"And?"

"I had better manifest my yang nature if I want a band, because I want the best musicians, not the first musicians."

"Then that's it. Set up interviews with — where do you want to start?"

"Guitar players."

"With guitar players at your place. Have real appointment times. Interview — how many can you see in a day?"

"Maybe six. I could spend an hour with each one."

"Six. Do you have six in mind already?"

"I do. I've been keeping my eyes open. I have at least six."

"All right. You'll have six guitar players come out to the ranch. Now, describe to me your yang plan for interviewing."

Mark nodded. "I get it. That was a trap. It isn't a yang plan at all, is it?"

"No! What is it?"

"A good plan made up of both yin and yang. Or, to put it simply, a good plan."

"That's exactly right. When you get it together, yin and yang vanish."

"This is very cool."

He had a thought.

"Can you come out and watch the interviews? I don't need you to do anything, and it isn't for moral support. I just think it would be interesting — useful — to debrief afterward."

So it happened that in early December I drove across the Golden Gate Bridge to Marin. Mark's ostrich farm sat near the coast in gorgeous rolling country dotted with organic farms, geodesic domes, and retreat centers. I pulled in past the ostriches, huge, prehistoric-looking creatures, and parked beside a stand of red oleander.

"I made an ostrich egg frittata," Mark said by way of greeting. "One egg is all you need. The frittata is a sop to yin."

He had also made a schedule and some rules for himself. Among the rules were that showing up late counted against you but didn't rule you out, since getting lost in this part of Marin was easy; that drug use (however it came up) counted against you but didn't rule you out, since that would rule out too many excellent musicians; and that under no circumstances would he indicate that he had accepted someone for the band at the end of their time together. His pledge was to say, "Thank you" and, "I'll get back to you" and nothing more.

"What are you looking for?" I asked.

"Musicianship. Energy. That extra something. A little greatness. A look. God — "

"It's a lot! But you aren't deciding on the spot. And who knows, it may be obvious."

"This is not fun."

"What's necessary and what's fun are two different things."

The long day commenced. First came a young man with long hair who played the guitar like lightning. Second came a black woman with a gorgeous, husky voice who played as well as she sang. Third came an old hippie who wasn't quite all there. Fourth came a young woman with tattoos and a hard edge. Fifth came a clean-cut musician you would take for an architect or an accountant.

Sixth came a biker who remembered Woodstock — the *original* Woodstock. Mark jammed with each of them in turn. Each could play. Each was a real musician.

At the end of the day we had a beer and sat on the porch. The ostriches cavorted.

"I've been fearing that all my life," Mark said. "And it was fun. It was great! What the hell have I been worrying about?" As an afterthought he said, "Will you take some frittata home with you?"

"How yin."

"Take some damned frittata!"

"How yang."

We laughed as the sun set over the Pacific.

SKILL FIVE

GENERATING MENTAL ENERGY

Many people who hope to create seem to lack the energy. They have a ton of energy for their tennis game, their shopping spree, or their poker night, but as soon as they think about the novel they intend to write they find that they need to take a nap. What are they experiencing? What does a person mean when she says, "I'm too tired to write" or, "I just don't have the energy to create"? As a creativity self-coach, you are obliged to understand the relationship between energy and creativity.

It's a straightforward matter to comprehend how we turn nutrients into energy and generate the power we need to perform tasks like breathing or chopping wood. We understand that we need food to live, and we recognize the causal relationship between our energy surge and the energy bar we ate a few minutes ago. We have a clear understanding that when we use the word *energy* in this context we mean the kind of physical phenomenon that explains why a lumberjack needs four thousand calories a day and a dieter wants fewer than fifteen hundred.

That's the simple part.

What about a phenomenon like the "low energy" of depression? What about the "high energy" we associate with arousal, passion, excitement, and enthusiasm? We know, for instance, that meaninglessness is an "energy drain" and meaningfulness is an "energy boost," but what does that say about the relationship between meaning and energy? We surely aren't talking about anything like strict caloric calculations. No simple model explains the energy of our emotional, psychological, existential, or creative life.

Consider that it takes extraordinary energy, an amazing stubbornness, and iron-willed determination to be anorexic and to starve yourself to death. You refuse to eat; you get weaker and weaker; you exert the tremendous mental energy needed to ward off the efforts of doctors, therapists, friends, and family members imploring you to live. You are a veritable dynamo in the service of your own death. You can't let down your guard, or they may feed you intravenously; you can't let down your defenses, or you might encounter the anger and pain inside; you can't be anything but vigilant, or you may lose your will to starve. Where is this tremendous energy coming from?

Let's take another example. A boy is jittery, restless, full of energy, and unable to concentrate in his fifth-grade classroom (although he is perfectly able to concentrate on his video games at home). People around him point a finger, and he receives a diagnosis of "hyperactive attention deficit disorder." He is therefore medicated. What medication does he receive? Ritalin, a stimulant! Physicians, at a loss to explain why you would give a stimulant to someone diagnosed as hyperactive, are obliged to call this a "paradoxical treatment" or a "paradoxical intervention."

But there is nothing paradoxical about the treatment if we make a distinction between physical energy and mental energy. The boy's physical hyperactivity is a function of his mental inactivity. He is thinking about too little — too little interests him, too little engrosses him — and this boredom causes him to bounce off the walls. He has an enormous need to be physically active precisely because he lacks mental stimuli and the mental energy that would follow from mental stimulation. The Ritalin stimulates this mental energy, allowing him to focus and concentrate, thus reducing his need to jump around. Suddenly there is no paradox. The artificial stimulation of mental energy reduces his need to expend physical energy.

If it seems strange to you that it requires mental energy to sit still or to starve yourself to death, think of the mental energy required of you not to scream, "Stop this, already!" in a boring meeting or not to blurt out, "Say something, already!" at a tedious lecture. We know that we are using up real energy in such situations and that the energy we are expending is mental, not physical. Such events mentally exhaust us and can prevent us from return-ing to our regular work. We use up our whole store of men-tal energy doing nothing more physical than not leaving the conference room or lecture hall.

We require mental energy to do everything from not leaving a lecture to writing a symphony. A person who actively makes meaning is obliged both to generate more mental energy and to expend more mental energy than someone who settles for received wisdom. When we say that a person is powerful, passionate, charismatic, ener-gized, and so on, we are making note of mental energy made visible, a wattage as real as that of the sun. An active meaning-maker is powerful, just as the sun is powerful, and for the same reason: the processes at work produce power.

In learning the skill of generating mental energy, our first axiom is that you generate this energy in accordance with the interest you take in some aspect of life. If that aspect is your body image, you will generate a ton of energy in support of your anorexia. If that aspect is your symphony, you will generate a ton of energy in support of composing. Your concerns produce mental energy, and the intensity of your concerns determines how much energy will be produced. Nutrients produce physical energy; inter-est, curiosity, desire, concern, and analogous mental states produce mental energy. The mind *makes* mental energy.

Mental activity *requires* — and then *uses up* — mental energy. It takes mental energy to think, to imagine, to calcu-late, to fantasize. It also takes a real expenditure of valuable mental energy to maintain half-hearted beliefs, to ignore important truths, to procrastinate, to not pursue your dreams. Keeping a defensive lid on life is real work and a real energy drain. No one mentally tires out more completely than the person who knows she ought to make meaning in a certain way but refuses to do so, unless it is the person who wages internal war about whether it would be better to pursue this or that meaning-making route.

Physical energy has to do with the way the body processes fuel and with human needs arising from our physical rootedness in the world. Mental energy has to do with the way the mind views the world and with our human need for meaning. Hard work is a physical energy drain, and a good night's sleep is a physical energy boost. A rejection letter is a mental energy drain to a writer, and an acceptance letter a meaning spark and mental energy boost. Over time, as science has advanced, we have learned how to talk sensibly about the domain of physical energy. Now, as a creativity self-coach, you must do the same in the domain of mental energy.

EXERCISE 9

Contemplating Mental Energy

You have three questions to answer for yourself. The first is, "What generates mental energy?" The second is, "What saps mental energy?" The third is, "What replenishes mental energy?" What kinds of answers are you looking for? Ones like the following: "desire," "fear," and "courage."

Or "curiosity," "doubt," and "hope." Or "passion," "complexity," and "clarity." Write at least a paragraph in answer to each of these three questions.

How, as a creativity self-coach, can you increase your mental energy? One powerful way is by cultivating positive obsessions and by eliminating negative ones. A positive obsession is a passionately held idea that serves your meaning-making needs. A negative obsession is a passionately held idea that serves no good purpose. Both generate a ton of mental energy, because passion generates mental energy. Both also expend a ton of mental energy. That is fine with regard to positive obsessions: you create like a wild woman, and then you rest. Every negative obsession, however, comes at a terrible cost; too many negative obsessions preclude even the possibility of creating. To increase the mental energy available to you, you cultivate positive obsessions and eradicate negative ones.

The idea that obsessions come in two flavors may be new to you, since common psychiatric wisdom has it that all obsessions are negative. Irrespective of their content or meaning, obsessions are viewed by mental health professionals as symptoms of obsessive-compulsive disorder or of some other disorder and as phenomena to be eliminated. Because they define obsession as an "inappropriate, unwanted, intrusive, recurrent thought," they leave themselves no room to consider the possibility that an obsession might be intrusive and recurrent but also appropriate and wanted.

Mental health professionals have talked themselves out of the chance to discuss the important differences between positive obsessions and negative obsessions by defining away the possibility that some obsessions might in fact be desirable. In 1877 the German psychiatrist Karl Westphal defined obsession in the following way: "Obsessions are thoughts which come to the foreground of consciousness in spite of and contrary to the will of the patient, and which he is unable to suppress although he recognizes them as abnormal and not characteristic of himself" (quoted in Ian Osburn, *Tormenting Thoughts and Secret Rituals: The Hidden Epidemic of Obsessive Compulsive Disorder* [New York: Pantheon Books, 1998]). If only he had called these particular intrusive thoughts "negative obsessions" and not "obsessions," the door might have remained open to a more rounded examination of this vital subject.

Negative obsessions, like fearing that your door isn't locked (and checking it a hundred times a day) or fearing that your hands aren't clean (and washing them over and over), are indeed a horror. No one would want them, and no one needs them. Positive obsessions, by contrast, are the fruit of our meaning-making efforts. Without them, life is dull, dreary, and meaningless. Because we rarely consider the distinction between positive obsessions and negative ones, we've thrown the baby out with the bath water and missed the chance to think about the value of positive obsessions — and about what might help us nurture and cultivate them.

Creators intuitively understand the difference between positive and negative obsessions. The visual artist Rosemary Antel, for instance, explained in an email to me:

> There are both positive and negative obsessions and I have experienced each of them. Positive obsessions are forward-looking. They point to future actions like tomorrow's painting or some other activity that I expect will be pleasurable and engrossing. These thoughts are characterized by feelings of competency and ability, even power. The thoughts are outward-directed, about things other than me, and lead to excitement and energy.
>
> Negative obsessions, by contrast, are backward-looking. The thoughts that chatter are replays of bad decisions, bad experiences, disasters, etc. The situation that I replay was grim or worse, either physically or emotionally. These thoughts are characterized by feelings of incompetence, stupidity, or powerlessness. The thoughts are inward-directed, all about me, and lead to depression and exhaustion.

In an email the abstract painter Aleta Pippin echoed Antel's sentiment:

> Good obsessions seem to be our life force. They inspire and motivate us forward. They are our reason

for getting up in the morning. They feel joyful. True, there are times when we are also frustrated by these good obsessions, but that passes. The frustration is usually the result of feeling that we aren't doing enough, or that we are currently unable to reach the quality to which we aspire. When good obsessions become our focal point, they lead us to success.

The most significant thing about bad obsessions is that you feel guilty, not good enough, that you don't measure up. They are based in fear and we use them as tools for self-flagellation. In fact, they will prevent us from moving forward and achieving our goals, because of the attention we give to them. They can become our negative focal point, preventing success.

One young artist explained, "I am a recent graduate of the Rhode Island School of Design. For many years the people outside of the art world have been telling me that my obsessiveness is not healthy. They don't understand that in order to succeed in creating anything you need to be obsessed!" This healthy obsessiveness is an attitude. You give yourself permission to love your own projects, your own ideas, your own creative impulses. This permission instantly unleashes mental energy. If you want to generate significant mental energy in support of your creative life, the place to start is by positively obsessing about a creative project.

EXERCISE 10

Cultivating Positive Obsessions

Bring your current creative project to mind. If you aren't currently engaged with a project, commit to the intervening step of choosing a meaningful project to work on. With your project in mind, say, "You *fascinate* me." Say, "You are *so* intriguing." Say, "I am *dying* to work on you." Say, "I am getting *so* excited." Say, "I've *got* to see how you turn out." Say, "I'm going to think about you *day* and *night.*" Say, "I have *no doubt* that this will be a rich experience." Say, *"Full speed ahead!"* Are you getting the picture? Get passionate. Obsess!

This lesson only scratches the surface of the subject of mental energy. Please continue your own investigations, since nothing is more important to your creative life than producing and renewing the requisite mental energy to create. The story that follows continues our brief examination of this territory by looking at one profound (and often dangerous) consequence of unleashing tons of mental energy. That consequence has a familiar name. Can you guess what it is?

Vienna, Austria

As it happens I am spending a few days in Vienna, whose sausages I sometimes crave. There I contemplate Beethoven and the dynamics of human energy.

Imagine a painter. She has become very excited about her current project. She prefers to work on it than to pursue her other activities. To use the language of the preceding lesson, she is positively obsessed. She recognizes that she is letting other things slip through the cracks as she works feverishly on her painting, but nothing feels important enough to cause her to stop.

She understands that she is operating in a self-absorbed, grandiose, arrogant way, as if that were anybody's business. Interruptions irritate her. She feels a constant, intense internal pressure to paint. Every so often she fantasizes about the glorious reception her painting will receive when it's finished and seen by others, a fantasy that exacerbates her high-strung state. She sleeps fewer hours than usual as, driven to create, she works on her painting late into the night and returns to it early each morning.

She feels both elation working so intensely and impatience that she can't work even faster. She experiences a heightened sexual energy that sends her impulsively on the prowl as well as bouts of anxiety when the thought strikes her that she may ruin her painting or complete it and hate it. Hovering nearby is a depression generated by the half-conscious fear that painting is not nearly as meaningful as she is making it out to be. Her thoughts race, both when she paints and when she's away from her painting.

Our painter — let's call her Mary — begins to notice that she is taking some unusual painterly risks. She discovers that she has thrown aside her quiet palette and is suddenly painting with brilliant colors. She feels an unusual lack of inhibition and an irritation with constraint that cause her to hate the feel of her clothes, so she begins to paint half-dressed. She experiences an increased talkativeness that causes her to call a certain painter friend two or three times a day to share her excitement, calls that she tends to make very late at night and very early in the morning. If asked, she would call herself wired, excited, anxious, edgy, ecstatic, pressured, elated, wild, and also uneasy and on the verge of a depression.

What does this picture look like?

Textbook mania, of course. My description of Mary contains every symptom of mania that clinicians use to diagnose the "illness" of mania. I am using quotation marks because mania ought not to be called a biological disease or a mental illness in instances like the one I just described. The putative symptoms of a disease that Mary is displaying are much better thought of as the consequences of a state that she herself has induced by her intense desire to make meaning. Her wild energy surge is existential, not pathological.

We are used to thinking of mania as an illness because the people tasked with the naming of diseases have dubbed it as one. The textbook definition of mania is "an episode of affective illness in which the predominant features are elevation of mood and mental and physical hyperactivity." If you go on a painting jag and remain in good spirits while you create, you are ill. We are certain that you are ill because you manifest elation, increased energy, a decreased need for sleep, racing thoughts, feelings of self-importance, sociability, a desire to embark on goal-oriented activities, extreme excitement, and high enthusiasm. Is calling this a disease a reasonable conclusion? Why should elation, increased energy, and a desire to embark on goal-oriented activities be considered signs of illness, as opposed to signs of excellent health?

We should reclaim the word *mania* and return it where it belongs, to the territory of meaning and the energy that accompanies our meaning-making efforts. Then we could begin to make some useful distinctions, for instance, between those manias in which the energized artist retains a grip on her mind and those in which she cracks. The latter is awful, a terror. The former is a state that we actively invite if we intend to create.

Let's dub Mary's state "mediated mania." In mediated mania a person retains control of her life and her mind even though she is hurtling along at breathtaking speed. She hasn't retained perfect control, and she herself can feel the risks she is entertaining by encouraging this manic state, but the risks feel worth it. Better to rev herself up in pursuit of meaning-making, she reckons, than to docilely accept meaninglessness. In a way, she has no choice: if it is crucial that she create, it is also crucial that she find the energy to create. She might as well hope to bake cookies without turning on the oven.

Experience has taught her that she can modulate, interrupt, or come down from her mania through specific strategies, like taking a hot shower or resting in a darkened room, two traditional home remedies for mania. Likewise, she can just grin and bear the state and wait for it to pass. She is manic, she knows it, and she lives with it, because she recognizes that her mania is a state that she herself has induced by pouring energy into the engine of her art. She has done it; she accepts it; now she must survive it.

You experience mediated mania when you cultivate positive obsessions and throw yourself body and soul into your work. You hurtle toward a destination, you permit your mind to race, you allow yourself to get excited, but you remain at the controls. Your control may be less sure than you would like it to be, since your rapid journey is unbalancing and even unhinging, but the control you retain is sufficient to allow you to return from the brink. That, at least, is your hope and your prayer!

If you can't return from the brink, if you hurtle off the tracks, your mania is no longer mediated. You have crashed and cracked. The difference between a mediated mania and an unmediated one is the difference between an intact egg that is being wildly shaken and an egg that cracks on the pavement. Mediated mania tosses the egg but doesn't break it. Unmediated mania cracks the egg wide open.

Leonard Woolf described the difference between Virginia Woolf's mediated manias, which could be controlled with isolation in a darkened room and bed rest, and those terrible manias, accompanied by auditory and visual hallucinations, that required hospitalization:

I am sure that, when she had a breakdown, there was a moment when she passed from what can be rightly called sanity to insanity. On one side of this line was a kind of mental balance, a psychological coherence between intellect and emotion, an awareness and acceptance of the outside world and a rational reaction to it. On the other side were violent emotional instability and oscillation and a refusal to admit or accept facts in the outside world. Four times in her life the symptoms of mania would not go away and she passed across the border which divides what we call insanity from sanity. (Quoted in Thomas Caramagno, *The Flight of the Mind: Virginia Woolf's Art and Manic-Depressive Illness* [Berkeley: University of California Press, 1996])

One distinction is between mediated manias and unmediated manias. A second is between the positive and negative aspects of any mania. On the positive side is the fact that you are intensely, passionately, energetically creating. On the negative side is the possibility, verging on a certainty, that you will treat the people around you roughly and poorly. Consumed by your racing thoughts, hungry to get your work done, rushing along at a hundred miles a minute, self-absorbed, arrogant, and grandiose, you are as likely as not to experience other people as irritations and obstacles. This brings us to Vienna and Beethoven.

A friend of Beethoven's observed, "Often, with rare endurance, he worked at his compositions on a wooded hillside and his work done, still aglow with reflection, he would not infrequently run about for hours in the most inhospitable surroundings, denying every change of temperature, and often during the heaviest snowfalls." Another friend recalled, "During his entire visit to Baden he was uncommonly gay and at times most amusing, and all that entered his mind had to come out. His talk and his actions all formed a chain of eccentricities, in part most peculiar. Even his tirades were surely only explosions of his fanciful imagination and his momentary excitement."

A student of his reported, "When he entered the room after our walk he ran to the pianoforte without taking off his hat. I took a seat in the corner and he soon forgot all about me. Now he stormed for at least an hour with the beautiful finale of the sonata. Finally he got up, was surprised to see me, and said, 'I cannot give you a lesson today. I must do some more work.'" Beethoven reported about himself, "I live entirely in my music; and hardly have I completed one composition when I have already begun another. At my present rate of composing, I often produce three or four works at the same time."

Another friend of Beethoven's observed, "Nothing can possibly be more lively, more energetic than his conversation when you have succeeded in getting him into a good humor. But one unlucky question, one ill-judged piece of advice, is quite sufficient to estrange him from you forever." This friend continued, "All in all, he is a dear, good fellow. Only his variable humor and his violence where others are concerned often did him a disservice" (Michael Hamburger, ed., *Beethoven's Letters* [New York: Dover,

1972]). Too many times Beethoven allowed playful pranks to turn ruthless and cruel, friendly moments to switch, in the blink of an eye, into rageful ones, pleasant conversations to devolve into tirades. He was a master, of course, and also something of a monster.

I sit outside at a café on Vienna's main pedestrian street and have a slice of Sacher torte and a double espresso. People hurry by, but none look obsessed. There is no one about to mistake for Beethoven. His passion to create, his need to make meaning through composing, and his relentless obsession with music wound him up like a top and produced a mania of mighty proportions. Beethoven made music like a great generator makes electricity; and he ran roughshod, out of control, over friends and strangers alike. It is a wild but not a pretty picture.

I am asking you to become more passionate and positively obsessed, to ignite your creative fire, to manifest the energy of a live wire. That is the message of the previous section. The message of this section is that there are consequences to the production of passion. That isn't to say that you should live mildly so as to avoid the ravages of an unmediated mania. No! — to live that way is to die. It is to say, however, that as your own self-coach you have the serious job of minding your mental state and reducing your speed around curves so that you don't fly off the tracks.

This is a strange lesson. It is a call to danger. It is a dare: find your passion, find your energy, ignite your being, and, in the process, risk mania. Should you accept this dare? It would be nice to know the odds. It would be nice to know if you really might induce a mania. It would be nice to know what sort of mania you might induce. Might you become a wildly passionate, endlessly productive person who maintains a grip on her mind and her life? In the absence of knowing for sure, what do you think? Certainly there is no dare more interesting to consider.

SKILL SIX

CREATING IN THE MIDDLE OF THINGS

eople do not create in a vacuum. In fact, in human affairs there is no such thing as a vacuum. People are born into this or that religion. They learn a certain language and are formed by that language. A war comes and changes everything; a drought comes and changes everything; menopause comes and changes everything. They must work, they must eat, they must deal with paying taxes and the images on their television screen and the values in their town. This is no vacuum!

Would-be creators are living people — New Yorkers, Egyptians, Catholics, lesbians — embedded in a particular culture and burdened with particular personalities. They have every manner of worry, doubt, and fear coursing through their systems and every manner of distraction pulling them away from the centering experience of creating. They have relationship pressures and day-job pressures stealing their neurons and preventing them from thinking deeply. They are *always* in the middle of life. There is no escape, no other way to be, no rest, no sanctuary.

When the Franco-Prussian war erupted, one Impressionist rushed to join the French Army and was killed. Another used his parental influence to avoid service. A third, without influence, fled Paris for the French countryside to paint in peace. All of them did something, even if that something was to bury his head in the sand. James Jones, having made his fortune from books like *From Here to Eternity,* thought to help some poor writers he knew by giving them enough money so that they could quit their day jobs and write. He gave them the money; they didn't write. Money was never the issue. *Everything* was the issue.

You must be able to create *in the middle of things,* or else you will not create. You must learn to take whatever practical and psychological actions are necessary to combat the anticreating forces that surround you and live within you. We only possess Newton's theory about planetary motion and about calculus because, terrified by the plague, he fled college and returned home to ride out the Black Death and to incubate his theories. Most of his fellow students died like flies. Dostoyevsky, his wife dying in the next room, poured his bitterness and emotional pain into the cynicism of the narrator in his existential classic

Notes from Underground. There is *always* profound tur-bulence within or without — that is life — and it is in the middle of that turbulence that you must create.

The Russian composer Shostakovich faced the collapse of his country, invasion by the Nazis, the horrors of Stalin, and death by the millions and composed three war sym-phonies. Not only did he compose them, he butted heads with Stalin, who demanded that he compose heroic, tri-umphant music. Shostakovich ignored Stalin, rounded up starving musicians, found instruments, put together full concerts attended by desperate souls dressed in rags, and fought a personal fight to keep up the spirits of his compa-triots. Could you have done the same?

Some determined artists weather even the most severe crises. But for most of us even ordinary, everyday crises stop us in our tracks. Most of these crises are internal, emotional, and existential, crises of faith and self-doubt, crises of self-recrimination and self-incrimination, crises of fear and meaninglessness. A marital spat or a single self-representation — calling yourself "untalented," say — is sufficient to keep a person from writing the book she may otherwise be close to writing. The "middle of things" that people are always in is, first of all, themselves: their own mind, their own inner conflicts, their own skin.

Sometimes it may *seem* as if nothing much is going on. You come home from work, have a little dinner, then turn on the television instead of turning toward the novel you hope to write. What exactly are you in the middle of there? Don't you have a "perfectly free" few hours in which to write? Absolutely not. To believe that just because you have no particular errands to run or duties to perform means that you are somehow not trapped in your own personality and your own culture is not to understand what being in the middle of things means. You are *always* in the middle of your personality, *always* in the middle of your stream of consciousness, *always* in the middle of your culture. There is no exit.

Unless you are impervious to the facts of existence — and no one is — you must learn how to create in the middle of things. You must learn how to create when wars are raging and when your hormones are raging. You must learn how to create even if you hate your country's policies or your own painting style. You must learn how to create even if you are embroiled in a bad marriage or living alone and lonely. You must learn how to create even if you work eight hours a day at a silly job or, sometimes worse, find yourself at home all day with time on your hands.

If you wait for a better time to create, better than this very moment, if you wait until you feel settled, divinely inspired, perfectly centered, unburdened of your usual worries, or free of your own skin, forget about it. You will still be waiting tomorrow and the next day, wondering why you never managed to begin, wondering how you did such an excellent job of disappointing yourself.

EXERCISE 11

Creating in the Middle of Things

How does a person manage to create in the middle of things? You must find your own answer to this question.

Please take all the time you need and answer this question: *How will I manage to create in the middle of things?*

How do most people meet this challenge? They don't. They don't create. A thousand things defeat them. One day it is this thing, the next day it is that thing; it is always something. Most people aren't as creative as they wish they were because they haven't mastered strategies for creating while life is going on around them. That is one sort of bad answer: not knowing what to do and not making the effort to find out.

A second bad answer is to *violently withdraw from life.* To reduce the things in which they are in the middle — like relationships — some creators and would-be creators slam the door on life. They manage to create in their hiding place, but at the very high cost of alienation, loneliness, and unhappiness. Whereas solitude is both necessary and beautiful in a creator's life, a violent withdrawal from life is a terrible response to this real predicament. Nor, of course, have they escaped, for they are still squarely in the middle of their personality, their thoughts, and a psychological place — because they are hiding and at war with life — which they experience as dark and difficult.

A third bad answer is to *sporadically and accidentally create,* that is, to only create when some fortuitous alignment of the spheres causes a creative impulse to course through you. You paint, then paint again two years or a decade later. You write eleven poems in your lifetime. You are always *wanting* to create, but you *actually* create only a tiny percentage of the time. This is as unacceptable an answer as the first two. You do not actualize your potential this way, and you disappoint yourself during those long stretches of time while you wait for your next flash of inspiration.

Not bothering to create, violently withdrawing from life in order to create, and sporadically and accidentally creating are all bad approaches. Well, then, what are some *good* approaches? We have been discussing them in each chapter. You get a grip on your mind. You articulate and then honor your life mission statement. You convince yourself that meaning must be made, not sought after or waited for. You learn how to generate (and modulate) your creative fires. You become an excellent creativity self-coach, someone who understands the rigors and contours of the journey and has learned how to rappel down cliffs and to ford raging streams.

An additional good approach is to have a repertoire of strategies available that actually work. Here, for example, are four tactics used by a creativity coach whom I trained:

"Suit up and show up."

Time-honored advice from AA can work for creating in the middle of things as well. Recovering alcoholics can't keep cutting work because they feel rotten or because they still haven't got their act together. Setting times to write and then showing up at the keyboard no matter what form the backbone of my writing strategy. "Suit up and show up" doesn't mean that it has to be pretty. I don't even have to feel prepared. I just can't afford any more excuses.

"Don't snivel."

A student from the University of Iowa's well-known writing program published an article in a slick magazine about the slogan taped to her computer. She said that "Don't snivel" embodied her whole creative philosophy. It's surprisingly powerful. Once you make the choice to cut off the pipeline of complaint, you free tons of energy. Not whining, not having to "process" issues was the single biggest aid in stopping my dependence on self-indulgent journal writing.

"Avoid anticipating."

Samuel Johnson repeatedly made the point that anticipation (or expectation) stood as the enemy of creativity. If I'm anticipating what fine and shining thing I will write, the first sentence I put on the page will blast my dream to bits. As I keep my writing appointments (a minimum of three each day), I write my first sentences without any expectation at all. Thinking how the mightiest river begins somewhere with a tiny, uncertain trickle, I'm unconcerned when my first sentences don't seem to roar.

"Imagine a flawless ignition system."

During moments before I write each morning (while feeding the cat and starting the coffee), I hold the picture of a car starting effortlessly on the first try. If I'm not already hearing my first sentences in my head, I'll savor the details of feeling a car key in my hand, turning it in the ignition, hearing a satisfying "vroom" as the engine fires. Since I can count on myself to start every morning, I'm simply less anxious and don't worry whether the road will be straight or not.

Here is a fifth tactic:

EXERCISE 12
Dropping Everything

I would love for you to learn how to drop everything and go create. The phrase "drop everything" means dropping your resistance, dropping your doubts, dropping those aspects of your personality that hold you down, dropping your nagging to-do list, dropping all the reasons that you and your efforts don't matter, *dropping everything* just as you would drop your parcels if your child got hurt or you would drop your clothes for spontaneous sex. I'm sure you get the idea — now go practice it! Drop everything right this minute and go write, paint, dance, sing, sculpt.

Greenwich Village, New York

I have come to New York in winter because a book of mine is up for an award and because my publisher is paying for the trip. I am a born-and-bred New Yorker and love New York, but I only visit occasionally. My publisher has put me up at the Hudson Hotel, a trendy place far hipper than I, and I wander the streets of Manhattan enjoying my old haunts and the bitter cold. I notice that the Russian Tea Room, a place that I sometimes took dates when I was eighteen, is closed and slated to become a golf museum. How strange.

I remember the Russian Tea Room's motto — "Just to the left of Carnegie Hall!" — which meant something to a leftist Jew like me whose friends' fathers had served in the Lincoln Brigade during the Spanish Civil War. I also remember a drink I used to order to impress my date, a Troika — vodka, Jamaican rum, and lime — which I had been looking forward to re-experiencing. Instead I have a Bloody Mary in the library bar of the Hudson Hotel, a room filled with art books and European accents.

My literary agent's office is in the East Village, and after our meeting I head toward Washington Square Park. It snowed the day before, and today is a gray, frigid, slushy day, a day I love because I know I am going back to California soon. People are bundled up against a bitter wind, and in Washington Square Park someone has set trash on fire in a garbage can to create some warmth. Several down-and-outers are gathered around the fire, including a skinny young couple sharing a container of steaming coffee.

Coming toward me is a man about my age who looks like he writes. His hair is a little too long, his clothes are unkempt, and he carries a small portfolio just the right size to hold some sheets of paper and a few pens. He is gnawing on a cheesesteak wrapped in paper, a beautifully messy sandwich that drips peppers and onions as he eats. Then — I can tell — he has a thought. He sits down on a wet bench, remembering at the last minute to use the brown bag from his sandwich as rear end protection. He opens his portfolio, wipes his hands on his pants, and writes.

I am just like him. I will eat something messy, wipe my hands on my clothes, and write. This nonchalant attitude toward messiness — and conformity, convention, seemliness — is a hallmark of those who actually create. What is in their mind is more important than what is on their hands. The wind may be bitter — they ignore it. The bench may be icy and wet — they sometimes remember to put down a brown bag. The only important thing is that they capture their thought.

There have been fastidious creators, men who wrote in pressed suits, women who meticulously organized their notes to the point of fetishism. The distinction I'm making is not between cleanliness and bohemian filth or between organization and disorganization. It is the distinction between having or not having permission to take your own thoughts seriously, one manifestation of which is that you write, draw, or compose the instant a thought arises, the moment you are moved to do so.

It is the distinction between creating in the middle of

things or not. As that pregnant thought passes, a would-be writer, someone uncomfortable with stopping everything for the sake of her own creative impulses, murmurs, "It would have been quite interesting to think about that. Oh, well." The practicing writer cries, "Where is the damned paper!" Either you create in the middle of things when ideas strike, or you don't.

I had a client named Harry, a sharp fifty-eight-year-old fellow who had worked for thirty years at a job that made little use of his intellect or creative abilities. Smarter and more knowledgeable than his colleagues, a dedicated classical music fan and film buff, he nevertheless had never followed through on his dream of writing a screenplay. He knew everything that the screenwriting guides had to say about plotting, pacing, dramatic arc, the hero's journey, character development, and so on; he had ideas for a hundred screenplays, but he had never come close to beginning.

He came to see me because of an unsettling experience. He and a well-known screenwriter had by chance attended the same charity event. They had struck up a conversation about the relative merits of Mozart and Beethoven, a subject my client could expound on until the cows come home. In the middle of their chat, which occurred as they were nibbling on chicken wings, the screenwriter got an idea. Rather than losing his train of thought and taking even a second to find a napkin and clean his hands, he wiped them on his good pants and scribbled his idea down. This act disturbed Harry no end.

Harry brooded about the screenwriter, the chicken wings,

the whole business. Finally he came to see me. What, he wondered, was his fastidiousness all about? Where had he learned that it was more important to be neat and proper than to record your fleeting ideas? What had caused him to despise messes? Harry hated what the screenwriter had done with a passion he knew was irrational. At the same time, he desperately wanted to be more like him.

What did I have Harry do? It won't take you three guesses. I brought in a hefty box of chicken wings, had Harry feast on them, and then had him wipe his hands on his pants. Ah, how he hated and loved that! What drama filled the room! I ate, wiped, wrote, ate, wiped, and wrote, modeling freedom. He ate, couldn't wipe, did wipe, couldn't write, did write, and so on, playing out the battle between fear and courage, between good habits that are bad and bad habits that are good, between creating instantly and waiting for a better, grease-free moment.

If courage didn't win a complete victory in the course of that chicken wing drama, neither did fear. Within days he had started a screenplay about Felix Mendelssohn and his sister, Fanny, an accomplished musician in her own right who had to play second fiddle to her brother. The ostensive villain of the piece was the father, who made it clear that Felix should manifest his genius and that Fanny should courteously entertain the guests. But the real villain of the piece? It was Felix, who needed his sister, loved his sister, used his sister, praised his sister, was endlessly supported physically and emotionally by Fanny, and who never championed her.

Harry worked on his screenplay for two months — but only sporadically, in dribs and drabs, a snatch of dialogue here, a camera direction there. Then he stopped writing altogether. He couldn't say why. He knew the Mendelssohn family better than he knew his own. He'd read everything about Felix and Fanny. He knew their world, their music, how they prepared their tea, what epidemics were most likely to cut their lives short. He knew everything, but he couldn't write. "I'm constipated," he said in the email setting up our next appointment. "I'll be on a trip for a few days, then let's meet."

He came to the café for his next session. "I went home to visit my mother," he reported. "She's in her eighties. We were sitting in the kitchen where I grew up. Back then she had a red-and-white enameled table that I can still picture vividly. We would have dinner in the living room, a formal meal that I hated, but I would always eat at that kitchen table after school, usually cookies that she had just baked, right out of the oven. You would think that would be a beautiful memory, something that Thomas Kincaid would paint and call *After School Blessing,* with light pouring in through the kitchen window."

He shook his head. "It isn't a beautiful memory," he continued. "She would wipe up the crumbs almost as fast as they fell from my lips. Her motto was 'cleanliness is next to godliness.' Something about that phrase always frightened me, and I had nightmares about witches on patrol for dirt. Everything got caught up in that relentless distinction between dirty and clean. Of course that's why my sock drawer is a paragon of virtue. Of course that's why I get my teeth cleaned more often than the ordinary mortal. Since nothing can ever be clean enough, orderly enough, safe enough, exactly what chance do I have?"

He didn't need to be told that he needed more than permission to make messes. He needed the equivalent of a bone marrow transplant, he needed to have his fear of mistakes and messes exorcised by the most powerful white witch in the Yellow Pages. Felix and Fanny resided in his brain, and if only he could let them chat, interact, and live, he would have his screenplay written. It would write itself. Instead, he monitored and censored his every move — his every potential wrong move. His history, translated into his personality, had a hammerlock grip on his ability to create, and that was that. He put his screenplay away, and when he retired watched a lot of foreign movies and listened to a lot of classical music.

My doppelgänger on the bench has finished his sandwich and his writing. He is a little blue from the cold, and so am I, on the opposite bench, where I too have been writing. He is content and satisfied; he's had his cheesesteak, he's used his pants as a napkin, he's written. I am possibly even happier than he is, because I still have my sandwich to look forward to. I can picture the shop on Bleecker Street that used to sell them, a shop next door to my favorite café of the old days, the Café Rienzi. I only pray that the cheesesteak shop is still there.

I am reminded of the epitaph that the Greek novelist Nikos Kazantzakis chose for himself: "I hope for nothing.

I fear nothing. I am free." Those are lofty goals, no doubt too lofty for most of us. To hope for nothing! To fear nothing! To achieve perfect existential freedom! It turns out that a much more modest goal — just growing brave enough to recklessly wipe our hands on anything handy — is lofty enough. It turns out that being able to create in the middle of things, the sticky spiderweb of our own personality first of all, is plenty.

My doppelgänger rises, sees a sparrow, and smiles. A cold sun has broken through the clouds. The sun is shining, and so are his pants.

SKILL SEVEN

ACHIEVING A CENTERED PRESENCE

As discussed in the previous chapter, you are obliged to create in the middle of things. What this means is that you must learn how to achieve a calm, centered presence even though you are feeling scattered, rushed, worried, depressed, anxious, or otherwise off-kilter. How can you pull off this feat? One way is by learning the technique I'm presenting in this chapter, which I call the Centering Sequence. It is a six-breath, six-thought, one-minute centering technique that I've tested with hundreds of volunteer subjects. It works. If you learn it and practice it, you will be able to grow calm and centered at will. As your own creativity self-coach, you owe it to yourself to try.

First you will need to become more aware of your breathing and learn how to breathe deeply. Although breathing deeply is the most natural way to breathe, in real life it is overridden by our shallow, rushed, everyday breathing patterns. The best way to arrive at deep breathing is to breathe naturally for several breaths, as preparation, then slowly deepen each subsequent breath until you feel yourself breathing deeply. With each long, deep breath you fill your lungs on the inhale, pause slightly, and slowly and completely exhale. Please do this now. Practice taking several long, deep breaths.

It is probably best if you do this while comfortably seated, with both feet planted firmly on the ground and your eyes shut. The first few times you try this you may notice that you're rushing yourself or that anxiety or stray thoughts prevent you from patiently inhaling and patiently exhaling. Try to consciously quiet your body and mind. This in itself is a centering activity. Grow calmer, feel a little more at peace, and see if your breathing progressively deepens. It most likely will.

If you're having trouble managing a long, deep breath, try counting to five on the inhale and five on the exhale. An unrushed, slow count of five or six should produce a deep inhale, and another count of five or six should produce a deep exhale. You may find that by filling up your lungs this fully you feel the need to rush the exhale. This may mean that you're straining and filling up your lungs too fully or that you need a little more practice in controlling the exhale. Take your time and continue practicing deep breathing until you feel you have it mastered.

Next, I'd like you to think of the inhale as one container and the exhale as another. On the inhale you think "half a thought," and on the exhale you think "the second half of a thought." For instance, if I were to ask you to think "stained-glass window," you would think "stained-glass" on the inhale and "window" on the exhale. Please give this a try. With your eyes closed, take a full inhale and think "stained-glass," then a full exhale and think "window," stretching out the word "window" so that it fills the exhale.

Try this exercise again but have as your goal not seeing any images. I've purposefully chosen a phrase that makes an image want to pop into your head, so you may have to do some work to prevent the image from appearing. It doesn't matter whether you succeed at this or not. The goal is for you to begin to sense the difference between thinking with accompanying images and thinking without any images.

It's very important that you break up a phrase so that it fits comfortably into each long, deep breath. For instance, try to think "stained" on the inhale and "glass window" on the exhale. I think you will find that breaking up the phrase that way is an awkward, if not downright unpleasant, experience. However, everyone is different, and you may find that the way I break up phrases is not the most natural way for you. Go with your way, since you are the one who must feel comfortable.

Consider a longer phrase, for instance, "a brisk walk in

the country." I think you will agree that it most naturally divides into "a brisk walk" on the inhale and "in the country" on the exhale. Any other division will likely feel awkward and unnatural. Try "a brisk walk in the country" in what I think is its most natural form, "a brisk walk" and "in the country." Then try some variations: say "a brisk" and "walk in the country" and "a brisk walk in" and "the country." Give this exercise a try right now.

It is also important that you learn how to completely fill each container (each inhale and each exhale) with half of the thought in question. This means that if I ask you to think "big dog," you will need to stretch the word "big" and the word "dog" to completely fill the inhale and the exhale. You would actually be thinking "biiiiiiig" on the inhale and "dooooooog" on the exhale, rather than "big" and "dog." Give this a try. Fill up your long, deep breath with "big dog," thinking an extended "big" on the inhale and an extended "dog" on the exhale.

Take a little time to think through what it means to divide the words of a phrase so that half the phrase fits naturally into the inhale and the other half fits naturally into the exhale. This will mean dividing the phrase appropriately, stretching out short words as necessary, running through a set of longer words a little more quickly, and sometimes even dividing words into their constituent syllables and sounds. (For instance, try comfortably filling a long, deep breath with the word *amazing*.)

For practice, break up the following phrases so that they naturally fill one long, deep breath:

"a meal with my brother John"

"a special meal with my brother John"

"a very special meal with my brother John"

"I am an artist"

"Paris, France"

"yes"

"I am perfectly fine"

"two toads and an alligator"

You will notice that some phrases are harder than others to break up into two equal components, generally speaking because they are too long or too short. For now, just register the fact that some phrases fit more easily into one long, deep breath and are more divisible between the inhale and the exhale than others.

EXERCISE 13

Breathing and Thinking

Before going on to the Centering Sequence, make sure that you've practiced the two preliminary steps described above, that is, breathing deeply and using the two halves of a breath as containers for holding thoughts.

The following are the six steps of the Centering Sequence. You will see that the first letter of each step, taken together, spell CENTER. This is designed to help you remember the sequence.

1. Come to a complete stop.

2. Empty yourself of expectations.

3. Name your work.

4. Trust your resources.

5. Embrace the present moment.

6. Return with strength.

The six thoughts associated with the steps of the Centering Sequence are the following. The parentheses indicate how these six thoughts are to be divided between the inhale and the exhale.

1. (I am completely) (stopping)

2. (I expect) (nothing)

3. ( ) ( )

4. (I trust) (my resources)

5. (I embrace) (this moment)

6. (I return) (with strength)

The parentheses for step three are empty because you need to choose the work you intend to name. What you insert as work is up to you. It could be (I am writing) (my novel),

(I am about) (to perform), or (I am feeling) (confident). Each time you use the Centering Sequence, you will need to begin by saying something to yourself like, "What would I like to designate as my work this time?" Alternately, you can designate one thing as "your work" for a period of time and consistently use that phrase. In either case, a complete sequence would look like the following:

(I am completely) (stopping)

(I expect) (nothing)

(I am becoming) (a real artist)

(I trust) (my resources)

(I embrace) (this moment)

(I return) (with strength)

or

(I am completely) (stopping)

(I expect) (nothing)

(I am off) (to write)

(I trust) (my resources)

(I embrace) (this moment)

(I return) (with strength)

or

(I am completely) (stopping)

(I expect) (nothing)

(I intend) (to stay calm)

(I trust) (my resources)

(I embrace) (this moment)

(I return) (with strength)

Step three of the Centering Sequence is the most interesting and intricate step in the process. Every time you use the Centering Sequence, you name the work you hope to accomplish the moment after you finish centering. This can be *"I will stay calm"* or *"I am returning to my novel,"* that is, you are naming the state you want to be in or naming concrete work you mean to tackle. Whatever you choose to name becomes an intention, a prompt, and a plan. There is great power in actually naming work you mean to undertake next, especially when you name it so mindfully.

The work you name can be the work you are about to do, like writing, painting, or cleaning out the closet; an intention, for instance, to write after work or to clean out the closet as soon as you get home from the supermarket; a quality you want to practice and manifest, like courage or patience; or the state you want to be in, like a calm state, an enthusiastic state, a centered state, a grounded state. You might name your work in any of the following ways and in countless other ways as well:

(I am returning) (to my novel)

(I am) (a real artist)

(I am working) (on my courage)

(Today) (I am calm)

(I accept myself) (completely)

(Big changes) (are coming)

(I will start) (my marketing)

(I am making) (that phone call)

(I am ready) (for that conversation)

(I am recovering) (my creativity)

(I will work harder) (than ever)

(I surrender) (to what is emerging)

and so on.

EXERCISE 14

Practicing the Centering Sequence

I would like you to experience the Centering Sequence now. I'm sure that you have an excellent, intuitive sense of what each step in the sequence is meant to accomplish and that you don't need any further instruction. Before you begin, name the work you intend to include in step three. Take a moment and ask yourself the question, "What would I like to think of as my work for the sake of this exercise?" When you have an answer, you are ready to begin.

If you can remember the six phrases, practice the sequence with your eyes closed, a good way to do this exercise. If you can't, practice it with your eyes open.

Remember, this is just your first experience of the Centering Sequence. You do not have to be an expert already!

Practice the sequence several times right now. Take your time and pay attention to the quality and length of your breaths. Remember that your objectives are to go through the sequence slowly, to take six long breaths, and to think the six phrases of the sequence as I have divided them up, one phrase per breath. Notice how you feel when you're done. If you feel more grounded and centered, make a mental note that you now have this straightforward centering technique available to you whenever you choose to use it.

Whether you employ the Centering Sequence, use some other technique (maybe gleaned from your meditation or yoga practice), or become centered and present without using any particular strategy, the task remains. Creating requires your centered presence. You must be present on stage, you must be present as you stand speculatively in front of your canvas, you must be present as you look deep inside for the right word to complete your poem. If you remain scattered, rushed, unfocused, and uncentered, you throw away your chance to create. As your own creativity self-coach, you will not let that happen.

San Francisco, California

I sit at my desk at six in the morning and watch the sun rise over San Francisco Bay. I'm actually looking southeast,

and the part of the bay I can see stretches between Candlestick Park (where the 49ers play and which has a new name
that no one uses) and the San Mateo Bridge, one of the links
between San Francisco and the East Bay and Oakland. I
overlook a working-class section of San Francisco and a
tangle of freeways, but it is all beautiful to the eye, which
should remind us how suspect beauty is. Isn't many a gorgeous sunrise the direct result of the worst air pollution?

I sit in San Francisco, but I communicate with the
world. That is what the Internet and email now permit. I
am working with two hundred volunteer subjects who are
practicing the Centering Sequence for a month. I send out
a daily lesson and await replies from Berlin, Bangkok, Boise,
Buenos Aires. Three-quarters of these artist-volunteers reside in the continental United States, and a quarter are far-
flung, bringing me news of the Bombay lamp trade
and the translating life in Tokyo. A creativity coach today
has the world as his oyster, which is wonderful and
remarkable. At six-thirty, the sky brightening, I send out a
lesson on "completing stopping," the first step in the
sequence. Here is that lesson:

> Today we take a look at step one of the Center-
> ing Sequence, "Coming to a Complete Stop." This
> step addresses a root cause of uncenteredness, our
> condition of perpetual flight. We are rushing
> around, prodded, poked, and pulled by our multiple
> duties and responsibilities. We are doing too many
> things and worrying about too many things. Many
> of us are also running away — from the awareness

that we are not living the life that we wish we were leading, not realizing our dreams, not doing our deepest work, not making sufficient meaning. So as not to notice these painful truths, we keep ourselves in mental and physical motion. The only tactic that can help us stop running is the demand we make on ourselves to stop running. We have to tell ourselves to stop. Either we come to a complete stop, or we rush headlong toward our next worry and our next depression.

If we fear that something is chasing us and wants to devour us, the only way we can learn that nothing is there is to stop and look. If we wake up in the middle of the night with the terrible feeling that someone is lurking in the corner, we dispel that notion by turning on the light, not by trying to talk ourselves out of our fear. When we come to a complete stop, we give ourselves the chance to see that many of our fears are smoke. They dissipate as soon as we stop running.

Other fears won't dissipate so easily. Still, if we are being chased by something that is as relentless and indefatigable as our worries, fears, resistance to self-awareness, and inability to do deep work can be, we will only exhaust ourselves if we keep running. We won't get free of our pursuers. Even if our fears are real, the only solution is to stop and confront them. The only way to slay some terrible self-accusation like "I am a fraud" or "I'm too ashamed to create" is to stop and hear it clearly. Only then can we reject it outright or do the inner work that will help make the accusation invalid.

You come to a complete stop by thinking "I am completely" on the inhale, pausing, and thinking "stopping" on the exhale. You want the experience of coming to a complete stop, not just the experience of thinking some words. If the words "I am completely stopping" do not produce a real sense of stoppage, you will not get full benefit from the sequence. It is like the difference between saying "I love you" and feeling nothing and saying "I love you" and having love well up within you. Open up to the feeling of completely stopping. Remember that you are aiming for a feeling here, not an idea.

If you do not believe in the idea of completely stopping, if you suspect that you fear stopping so much that you won't mean it when you say it, or if you can't quite grasp the concept, then it would be good if you did some preliminary work on practicing stopping. See if you can stop everything, even just for a few seconds. What you may hear yourself say after just a split second of trying this is "I need a drink" or "I hate this" or "I have too much to do" or "This is ridiculous." Try to replace any thoughts of this sort with "I'm not afraid of stopping" or "It's about time that I stopped."

You may want to make some notes to yourself about what thoughts and feelings arise in you when you try to stop completely. You may be meeting your darkest fears, your largest worries, your gravest disappointments. The remaining steps in the Centering Sequence are designed to reduce these fears and counteract these worries. You will see how these steps work in the coming days. For now, be brave and commit to really, totally, completely stopping when, as step one of the Centering Sequence, you think "I am completely stopping."

Please practice the Centering Sequence several times now, paying special attention to the first step in the sequence, completely stopping.

I send out this lesson and go about my business of writing and coaching. Somewhere in New Zealand someone is now trying to stop. So is someone in Chicago. And someone in Seattle. It is remarkable. By early afternoon the first volunteer responses appear in my email inbox.

Katherine, a painter in Maine, writes me:

My fear stands in the way of me completely stopping. Using the Centering Sequence, I felt calm and I felt some power, some kind of love (from God?) and curious expectation. I really need an inner voice that tells me to stop and to center myself. I have been on the run all my life. I have been on the run from myself and the trauma I carry since my childhood. My own existence reminds me of this trauma, so therefore I am on the run from myself. But it is no longer a good solution to run from boyfriends, jobs, apartments, tasks, everything. This really must change, and I think that maybe it can if I truly commit to using the Centering Sequence.

Kristin, a songwriter in Queens, writes:

I take this step to mean that I am stopping all thought and activity and becoming aware of the present moment. I am not doing, simply being. I am putting aside all distraction and paying attention to what's going on inside me. What usually gets in the way of me completely stopping is a compulsion to "get things done" or my running away from something that is difficult to face or experience. For a few moments using the sequence, yes, it was quite a relief. But it wasn't long before I was interrupted by thoughts of all the things I "should, need, or want to be doing." I have much more work to do on this!

Sam, a stand-up comic in Atlanta, writes:

I take this step to mean not just temporarily setting aside the endless to-do list of aspiration and work and daily life, but truly believing that the present moment is already good, that there is no need for it to be improved upon or altered. What stands in the way of me completely stopping is a sense that work and life are a treadmill moving faster and faster, that standing still means falling behind. There is also a sense that I should be more than I already am, which is a feeling that dissolves when you examine it and you see that it's based on nothing and means nothing.

Practicing the Centering Sequence today, I was able to experience a complete stop. I had been feeling tortured today, a familiar but baseless feeling that more and more work is always needed, that everything good will evaporate if I stop for a moment, that there is not a moment to lose. To insist on stopping, to sit still and look head-on at that awful feeling, shows it up for the sham that it is. I had to accept that nothing is on the verge of collapsing and that thinking so is just a habit of being. This is great!

Next comes an email from Rome. Gabriella, a painter, writes:

Why do we avoid stopping completely? What stands in the way most often is my mind, which is usually like a rubber suction cup on everything around me: my husband and his moods, my job, the cats, the dirty laundry, telephone and email messages to return, "whose birthday is it this week?" and things like that. Mostly, I don't stop completely because I don't want to stop being "me" — as though there is a certain amount of psychic focus required at all times to maintain my identity.

Overall, I am finding the Centering Sequence very valuable. But a lot of childhood is surfacing, and I feel the impulse to scream. I also wonder, are we sure that stopping completely isn't like dying? I think it is like dying. And we're all terrified of that. So it looks like it's *not* an easy thing to want to stop completely. But wait — it's the part of me that gives up easily that is saying that. Well, these ramblings are very strange and are coming from a part of me that I'm usually not supposed to talk about. This is both excellent and very scary.

In comes an email from the wilderness. Jody, a novelist, writes:

Completely stopping had no meaning for me until two years ago, when I moved away from San Diego and the life I had created there, a hectic, unhappy, unfulfilled, empty life. Finally I had the guts to leave a tenured position with benefits and retirement. I knew if I stayed I would not live to use the retirement. Here I am today, living in a cabin built in 1937. My day begins with looking outside where there is a forest with all the trimmings: beautiful deer, wild rabbits, coyotes, trees, fresh air.

To me, completely stopping means that I open

the curtains in the morning and stop, look, listen, hope, pray, laugh, but mostly listen for my own voice, the one I have distrusted for soooo many years. Completely stopping means trusting non-motion, nonactivity, nonthinking (almost), and listening to my world. Now, using the sequence, I feel like I am going into myself and somewhere beyond, or maybe it's pulling me toward a place I have not been before. Fortunately, I have prepared for the last two years for this. I am ready to completely stop. I don't think I was before.

Susan, a sculptor in Oakland, writes:

I find it difficult to stop. I have a tendency toward what Buddhists call "monkey mind." It's always distracting me and haranguing me. I have never been overly successful at meditation as a result of monkey mind, but there are times when I manage a little silence and follow my breath down into my body and find some measure of peace and "stoppage." But the monkey keeps pointing to the next step and saying go on, go on, next! I am hoping that it is just a matter of practice.

I have fought long and hard with myself not to think of stopping as a negative. Stopping for me now is about surrendering, about being in the present and letting go of thoughts of the past and the future. It is also about being quiet, still and inside my body. We spend so much of our day in a "from the neck up" mode that it is both a shock and a joy to get back into the body. I think that there really is something to the idea that we are spiritual beings trying to learn how to live in the physical body, as opposed to human beings trying to learn how to be spiritual. Stopping is a part of all this.

The emails continue to arrive all afternoon and into the night. Around the world, a few hundred people are trying to center, to get a grip on their minds, to achieve presence, to do their art. Before the Internet, it would have been impossible for a lone individual to communicate daily with a population worldwide. Now a creativity coach like me can do just that — effortlessly, sitting at his desk, watching the morning fog lift over the Oakland hills.

SKILL EIGHT

COMMITTING TO GOAL-ORIENTED PROCESS

ou start to write a novel. You begin with enthusiasm and then, within a few days, as Virginia Woolf put it, "resignation sets in." You resign yourself to the unhappy fact that your novel will not just flow out of you, as if you were taking dictation from your muse. You realize that you know what your novel is about much less than, in the first glow of enthusiasm, you thought you knew. Now, on top of not knowing, you have actual sentences and paragraphs to deal with, sentences and paragraphs that you do not love. Yes, it is early; yes, this is a draft; yes, the beauty will appear in the revising. Yes, this is the process. But you hate it.

Sometimes hating your novel is part of the process. That is not a cosmic joke to rail against. It just is. You will sometimes actually hate the process of writing your novel even as you fully understand that there can be no other process, no way around it. This disliking, this worrying, this fearing the worst, this plodding rather than soaring, all this is sometimes part of the process. You must accept this truth.

You can choose to say, "I can do this even though it hurts." That honors the process. Or you can dishonor the process by fantasizing that it must be different for luckier mortals. You can suppose that some writer somewhere, whom you envy and hate, is dashing off beautiful page after beautiful page, turning out masterpieces with ridiculous ease, laughing all the way to the computer and back, doing his effortless genius thing while you refuse to get out of bed. You can fantasize in this fashion to let yourself off the hook and avoid the reality of process. Don't.

You may want the process to be otherwise. You may try to wait it out, wait for it to miraculously change, so that, for instance, roses bloom in winter, oranges drop from the tree already peeled, and your hearing and eyesight improve as you age. How long will you have to wait? A very long time. Yes, genetic engineers are probably working on your already peeled orange right now. Yes, some geezer somewhere is replacing his worn-out hearing aid with a much better one and finally hearing all the things that his relations have been saying, much to his dismay. You can try to speed up natural laws, reverse natural laws, manipulate the natural course of events. But first you must understand and embrace the reality of process.

One such law is that much of the time you are writing your novel you may not be pleased with it. Embrace that! Stop wishing it were otherwise. Stop avoiding nature. Stop hoping that reality were more like a pleasant dream. Stop craving the fantasy that you are a genius and that everything that flows from your pen will be honey. Embrace the reality that some of what you produce will be inspired, that some of what you produce will be dull, and that there will never be a substitute for showing up and moving your fingers over the keyboard.

Imagine planting a thousand seeds in a square foot of earth. How many will bloom? A few. The rule is, when many vie for limited resources, only a few survive. Think actors. Ninety-nine out of one hundred actors will not find work. If you put a hundred thousand actors in a city that needs only a thousand, what must the actor who wants to work prove to be? The exception. This isn't just a piece of rhetoric: she must literally *prove the exception.*

She must do more than the next actor. Yes, she must also get lucky, and luck is not just opportunity meeting preparation, luck is actually just luck. She must also have some spark, some light in her eyes, and if this isn't part of her constitution, that may be that. But if she has that light, she mustn't wait for luck. She must do everything in her power to prove the exception. If that means making a hundred phone calls a day, then that is exactly what she must do. This guarantees nothing, just as nothing guarantees that one of those seeds will bloom. It does, however, honor the reality of her circumstances and give her a better chance — maybe her only chance.

Part of her process is proving the exception. She doesn't do "what every actor does," as if that honored the process. Honoring the process is not the same as "doing what others in my field do." Honoring the process means picturing your goal, understanding what gets you from here to it, and tackling those tasks. One actor is taking a sword-fighting class, because it sounds like fun, a second is networking day and night with studio types whom she despises. Which one will find work? Even if the movie calls for sword-fighting, it will be the networking actor, don't you think?

EXERCISE 15

Thinking Clearly about Process

1. Get your discipline clearly in mind. (I'll use novel writing as an example, but substitute your own discipline.) In your mind's eye, picture the process of writing a novel from beginning to end. Include marketing the manuscript and promoting the finished novel. Picture the process as a movie you run in slow motion. Watch yourself write and do whatever else is natural to the novel-writing process, like sitting on the sofa not writing, jumping up from your writing to make popcorn because you need a break, strangling your parakeet because you really want to strangle your novel, and so on.

2. Next, ask yourself the question, "If I were to
    consciously set out to honor this process, would
    the movie look different?" Run the movie again,
    in slow motion, imagining this time that you are
    doing a better job of honoring the process. What
    is different this time? For instance, do you sit
    longer at your computer screen, do you get
    there at seven in the morning rather than at three
    in the afternoon, do you complain less to your
    mate about the fate of writers, do you stop the
    alcohol use, and so on?

3. Having watched both movies, write out an
    answer to the following four questions (remem-
    bering to substitute your own discipline):

•   "What does honoring the (novel-writing)
    process mean?"

•   "What do I currently do that dishonors the
    (novel-writing) process?"

•   "What new things would I like to do to honor
    the (novel-writing) process?"

•   "When I claim to be blocked or stuck or when
    I start calling myself or my (novel) bad
    names, what will I do that honors the process
    and gets me back on track?"

There are two profoundly different senses of process,
"goal-less process" and "goal-oriented process." Because

the former is infinitely easier to honor than the latter, a great many people choose the former and righteously argue that they have committed to process and that they are honoring it. In fact, they have used the word's multiple meanings as a way to evade their responsibilities as a meaning-making creature.

You would have a beautiful wild garden without lifting your finger if you accepted that you would love and call beautiful whatever appeared in your garden. This might mean that you would find yourself sitting at your window smiling at a tangle of overgrown weeds, but if your only objective was to "honor your garden's process," you would be right to smile. You have let your garden "do its thing," and no one can argue with you.

This is the epitome of "goal-less process" and is captured by phrases like "everything is for the best," "everything happens for a reason," and "it's God's plan." If, however, you wanted your garden to supply you and your family with food, it would not work to just sit there. It is conceivable that by some fluke your garden might be filled with self-tending fruit and nut trees impervious to age and disease; that is, you might have purchased a house attached to the Garden of Eden. More likely, if you sat there without cultivating your garden you would die of starvation, whispering, as you died, "No doubt there was a good reason I went hungry!"

Let's say that you wanted and needed to use your garden to grow produce to feed your family. What would change? Everything! You would have to answer the question, "What is the process of cultivation?" not, "What does my garden want to do on its own?" It would no longer amuse you that your garden only wanted to grow bamboo and crabgrass. You would have to get rid of the bamboo and the crabgrass in the service of your life mission, feeding you and your family. You would have to discover, with the help of experts at your garden center but mostly through trial and error, what your garden could support.

If your garden naturally supported squash, squash would be easy to cultivate. But what if you wanted white peaches? Then you might have to do a hundred things in support of helping your fledgling dwarf white peach trees survive, from making the soil more acid or more base to fighting off white-peach-eating bugs with your bare hands. This is so much less amusing than sitting at your window praising God for giving your garden bamboo and crabgrass. This is so much more like real work.

You wanted to learn creativity self-coaching because you wanted to manifest your potential and do the creative work you've always dreamed of accomplishing. These are goals. Since you have goals — and you do — you must surrender to the fact that a commitment to goal-oriented process, not goal-less process, is required of you. You can relinquish your goals, sit at your window, and marvel at the way weeds want to take over your garden. Or you can go out and weed. Both are "part of the process," but they are parts of different processes, only one of which serves you.

EXERCISE 16

Honoring Goal-Oriented Process

1. Describe in your own words the difference between goal-less process and goal-oriented process.

2. Write down the mission statement that you crafted in chapter 2. What is the relationship between goal-oriented process and your life's mission?

3. Under what circumstances will you honor goal-less process and under what circumstances will you honor goal-oriented process?

4. Are you comfortable with the idea of goal-oriented process? If not, what can you do to help yourself grow more comfortable? (Hint: Get a grip on your mind!)

5. Invent a ritual that honors goal-oriented process.

Paris, France

I have been invited to teach a weeklong workshop as part of the Paris Writers Workshop program. Each of four faculty members — a poet, a novelist, a short story writer, and me — will work with a group of twelve students intensely for five three-hour morning sessions. The pay is modest, but the offer provides an unbeatable reason for spending time in Paris, a place I love and hold as "part of the process."

That first Sunday afternoon I take the métro from the Marais to Montparnasse, to the headquarters of WICE, an acronym for Women's International Continuing Education, the group sponsoring the Paris Writers Workshop. At this Sunday reception faculty and students meet each other and get the lay of the land. It turns out that three of the four workshops will be taught on-site and that the fourth will be held across the street in a room above a café. I want that venue! — but instead I am shown to a narrow room that is completely filled by one long table and thirteen chairs. It is cramped, but I don't mind. Cramped quarters are not a problem.

The leader of the poetry workshop, however, does have a problem. She is famous and has gotten the main room for her workshop, a room spacious enough that it is serving as the site for our reception. The largeness of the room is fine with her. Its location is the problem. She anticipates difficulties with me and my group because we will have to pass through her room when we take our breaks, which may disturb her poets. Internally, I smile. Ah, poets!

Well, let's coordinate our breaks, I suggest. We won't be taking any breaks, she replies. I think to myself, That is either wonderful or quite insane. Does honoring the process mean going three hours without peeing? In any event, I have the answer, albeit an ironic one. Well, take my room, I offer. Then no one will disturb you. As if she will agree to that!

She takes a peek at my small room and says, no, no, her room will serve her better. I smile. She drops her admonitions about our disturbance potential, but I know that her complaints are only hibernating. On Monday my group and I meet joyously in our small room and begin our work together. There is barely enough room for me at the far end where the erasable board lives. We have our coffee and banana bread, supplied by WICE, and babble. The unspoken message is "We are in Paris! This is good! Let us work!" Eventually we take our mid-morning break.

We are as quiet as mice as we pass behind the poets. Well, to tell the truth, maybe we are still talking a little. We are not loud and insensitive, just alive, and in Paris. Yes, we make a little noise! I know that I will be hearing about our boisterousness, and indeed I do, as soon as the morning session ends. The WICE coordinator is embarrassed to tell me that the poets have a bone to pick with us. We passed behind them so loudly that they could hardly think. Perhaps we can pass just a tad more quietly? "Of course we can!" I reply, quelling her fears that a battle is brewing. "We understand the needs of poets."

It turns out that I made an impression on one of my students that first morning. She calls up a friend who lives in Nice, a journalist who is struggling with a nonfiction project, and tells her, "Come to Paris this instant! Have a coaching session with this man." Two days later her friend — Susan, let's call her — arrives. The three of us meet early one morning at a café across Boulevard Montparnasse from WICE, a local joint called Le Chien Qui Fume

(The Dog Who Smokes). Surely it's worth a visit to Paris just for the café names! My fee for this impromptu creativity coaching session is a croissant and coffee, a modest fee even if you count the several refills.

Susan tells me her story. She has been an academic and a reporter and has thousands of pages of notes and materials gathered for a cultural and political examination of Latvia. Her problem is that she doesn't know what to do with all this material. She is certainly not experiencing her thousands of pages, these notes and articles and photocopied chapters of books that take up a full room of her apartment on the Riviera, as abundance. She would like to tell me about how she has gathered this material and why it will be of importance to readers, but I stop her. "How do you intend to organize this material?" I ask. Of course that is the question. It is the only honorable question to ask. It is the question that she has come from Nice to have answered. It is also the question she would like to address last, or not at all.

It is certainly human nature to gather and gather and then, because of anxiety, not to organize. It is exactly like piling treasures (and some junk) into your garage and then feeling unequal to cleaning the space. Nor is there any particular need to clean that space, until you want to sell your house and your real estate agent says, "Do something about that garage!" Susan has been collecting treasures to the point of overwhelm and has been avoiding the obvious: she needs to clean her garage. I am her real estate agent.

"How do you intend to organize this material?" I repeat.

How exquisitely she's been avoiding this question! She's been lamenting, worrying, complaining, writhing, medicating her headaches, collecting more treasures, but avoiding the only salient task in front of her. She says, "I don't know." She thinks she means it. I am convinced that she does know and that there is nothing but anxiety between her and her own good answer.

I say, "This won't be so hard. You've just built this up into a hellish task. Calm down and tell me, how would you like to organize your material?" She calms down. I watch her soften and begin to think. For the first time since she began this massive project, she looks her material in the eye. These aren't spiders and snakes, after all, just bits of information about Latvia! — and information doesn't bite. I watch her vanish into that trance state that signals a person is creating.

In a minute she returns from communing with her thoughts and begins speaking. By the end of our breakfast session she has three separate books planned, each one smart, each one manageable, each one on target. She hardly knows how to thank me. But there is only so much coffee I can drink. We shake hands and she rushes back to Nice to get started. I don't shout in parting, "This is how you honor the creative process!" But I might have.

My student and I leave The Dog Who Smokes and cross a rain-soaked Boulevard Montparnasse. It is two minutes to nine, and we will just make it on time to the morning session. We'll even be able to grab a slice of banana bread. As we push open WICE's massive doors we share a smile. It is time to make like mice and spare the poets any aggravation. We move as silently as ghosts behind the working poets, who have started early and are already attacking — I mean, critiquing — one of their own.

That afternoon I go shopping for fruit at an open-air market on the Boulevard Richard Lenoir. The prices are low — whole pineapples are 75¢ each, apricots are 40¢ a pound — and I decide to buy some apricots. I approach one of the fruit-and-vegetable stalls, arrive at a huge bin of fruit, and watch as the woman next to me selects individual apricots and puts them into a paper bag. I do the same, selecting the good ones and avoiding the bad.

The young Arab minding this long row of produce comes over to us, lectures the woman, hands her a scoop buried among the apricots, and orders her to use it. I don't know what the two of them are saying, but it's perfectly clear what he intends to communicate. "At these prices," he must be saying, "you don't get to pick just the good ones. You take the bad with the good. That's the deal."

She doesn't agree. She makes a "go away!" gesture, utters some choice words of her own, and keeps selecting the good ones. He chides her some more and, confronted by her stony indifference, throws up his hands. Then he turns to me. I scoop! But in fact it isn't to avoid a scene. The idea appeals to me. "Taking the bad with the good" is a principle that all creative people, and especially American ones, are apt to forget — and may never have learned in the first place.

In America, we are taught to expect only the best. In a

modern supermarket, everything looks perfect. This means that nothing is ever ripe — but the displays look so good! In a modern movie, the production values are beyond belief. The movie may be silly and beneath contempt — but it looks good! Where and when are we taught to "take the bad with the good"? Nowhere, not in a culture dominated by appearance over substance. Because of this we never learn what "honoring the process" means.

To create we have to take the bad with the good. We're bound to write bad paragraphs along with good ones. That's the eternal law. We can get rid of those bad paragraphs later on, but first we must write them. Otherwise we won't write anything at all. If we try to write only the good paragraphs, we are three-quarters of the way toward paralysis. The name that we've coined for this problem is "perfectionism." But it isn't that people afflicted this way are striving to be perfect. They are just striving to be good, which would be no problem at all, if only they also had internal permission to be bad.

How wonderful can our writing be if it is tied to the constipated idea that only gems must emerge from our pen? Imagining those gems is like imagining those perfect tomatoes piled high in a frigid supermarket, impervious to harm because of their genetically engineered leather skins. Take your cue from that bin of apricots, filled with rock-hard fruit, perfect beauties, and spotted leftovers. Just scoop. Scoop! It's a real character builder.

Honoring the creative process means organizing your material, making mistakes, spending a year on a book that may not work, getting an answer in the middle of the night and coming fully awake, struggling with a corner of your painting for a month, loving your sculpture in the morning and hating it at five o'clock — the list is very long. It is longer than your arm. On it are many, many disappointing realities. Also on it, however, are your beautiful successes and the truth of the matter.

Friday dawns. It is the last day of the workshop. In the morning we complete our work, and in the afternoon we gather for a party. There is a lot of cheese, and the fruit is uniformly good-looking. This fruit was not scooped! The poets hang together, as do we. The party ends, and we stream out into a gorgeous Paris afternoon. The métro would be quicker, but I decide to walk home. My studio is across the Seine, an hour away by foot. I head out and at the entrance to the Luxembourg Gardens am struck by an idea. I had better be a person of my word! To not stop and capture that thought would surely dishonor the process. I hurry in, grab a chair, and pull out my pad.

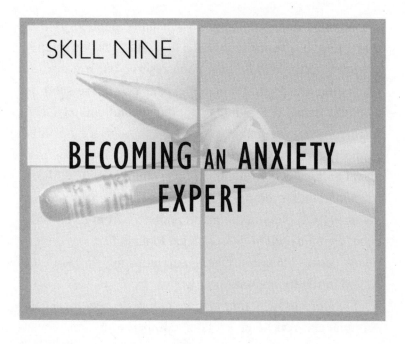

SKILL NINE

BECOMING AN ANXIETY EXPERT

nxiety prevents us from creating well and
sometimes from creating at all. Would-be creators are stymied more by anxiety than by any
other factor. It is most often anxiety that causes them to
choose one life over another ("Computer engineering feels
safe — living the artist's life feels *too* scary!"), one art form
over another ("I can knit, but painting feels *too* scary!"),
one locale over another ("I should probably live in New
York, but New York feels *too* scary!"), and keeps creating
off their daily to-do list ("Better that I do *anything* than that
scary creating!").

What is anxiety? Anxiety is usually defined as irrational fear. It is rational to fear a lion attack as you sleep in your tent in the middle of a lion preserve but irrational to fear a lion attack as you sleep in your bed in the suburbs. The first is fear, the pundits say; the second, anxiety. This distinction is reasonable enough on the surface but misleading when you take a second look. It certainly is irrational to fear a lion attack in the suburbs. Is it really so irrational, however, to fear potentially negative consequences from playing the piano poorly in front of an audience, trying to sell your book idea to an editor, or facing a blank canvas? Certainly not. Anxieties of this sort are rooted in reality and rationality.

Say, for instance, that you are hoping to become a concert pianist. You enter a major competition. The winner gets an international tour and the runners-up not much of anything. Is it irrational to suppose that not winning that competition will negatively affect your career? You win, you become a famous soloist. You lose, you end up teaching piano theory at university or, worse, away from the piano altogether. The competition *matters* to you. The competition is life altering, for both the winner and the losers. It is irrational to fear the consequences of this competition only if it is irrational to care whether you end up an international soloist or a telemarketer.

We get anxious when we fear for our future. We get anxious when we fear that our self-image is about to get tarnished. We get anxious when we fear that we might lose a year writing a novel that never sells or composing an opera that is never performed. We get anxious when we fear that our self-esteem, perhaps precarious to begin with, is about to receive a blow. We get anxious when we fear that we are about to embark on something with potentially negative consequences for our mental, emotional, physical, existential, or spiritual health. That is not irrational. That is the epitome of rationality.

Something as innocent-seeming as standing in front of a blank canvas and preparing to paint can bring up all these fears, which it is quite insulting to call irrational. Say, for example, that you are intrigued by the power of one-color paintings like Ad Reinhardt's all-black paintings or Yves Klein's all-blue ones. You decide that you want to work in that tradition by painting some all-red paintings. At the same time you harbor the half-conscious fear that your monochromatic painting won't sustain you emotionally or intellectually. You fear that going down that road constitutes a detour or, worse, the beginning of a lifetime of superficial work. You have the inkling that your attraction to monochromatic painting is as much a flight from going deep as a real love.

In this scenario, to begin your all-red painting is not just a waste of time but a step down a slippery slope. Somewhere inside you know this and experience anxiety. Maybe you experience it as a heaviness that physically prevents you from moving from your sofa to your studio, maybe you experience it as butterflies in your stomach that provoke many trips to the bathroom, maybe you experience it as a linguistic defensiveness that sounds like "I need a spare tube of cadmium red before I can begin my painting" or "I don't think I can paint on such a cloudy day." You have an inkling that you are about to make a mistake and you experience anxiety, which in this case we might call the "gift of fear" because your fear is well placed.

Consider a second scenario. You love the paintings of Reinhardt and Klein and are deeply fascinated by the power of monochromatic painting. At the same time you are surprised that, while red has been used more in the last hundred years than in the previous thousand, beginning with Matisse's virtually all-red paintings and continuing as a liberated, much-loved color throughout the twentieth century, no one has yet done for red what Reinhardt did for black. You understand that you want to go beyond monochromatic painting, that monochromatic painting is a stepping-stone on your journey and not your destination, but you feel that you won't be able to progress as a painter until you really learn what one color can do.

Still, you don't begin. Something is preventing you from starting. You don't quite recognize that anxiety is the culprit, and you don't have a good handle on the reason for your anxiety, that painting monochromatically is considered old-hat and fraudulent by so many painters and pundits that to create all-red paintings is to risk contempt and ridicule. Their opinions, though, ought to be of no concern to you, if you have rightly discerned that painting monochromatically is an important step on your journey. If anxiety was a "gift of fear" in the first scenario, it is rather more a "curse of fear" in this one.

In the first case your anxiety ought to be heeded, because you yourself do not believe that proceeding with monochromatic painting is a good idea. In the second it ought to be acknowledged, managed, and overcome rather than heeded, since monochromatic painting is a necessary link in the chain of your artistic growth. You can see from these two examples that anxiety is *not the enemy*. It is simply a vital feature of our early warning system against threats. Sometimes we want to heed that warning because the threat is real, and sometimes we want to ignore it because the threat is conjured. It is sensible not to enter an elevator with a stranger if we get a certain tingle down our spine alerting us to danger. It is equally sensible to fly off to Paris for the opening of our gallery show even though flying makes us anxious. In each case anxiety merely signals a threat, and *then the threat must be evaluated.*

Whether we heed or ignore a warning signal ought to be a decision based on our analysis of the situation, not a reflexive reaction to an uncomfortable feeling. If we reflexively ignore all such warnings, we become reckless and self-destructive. If we reflexively heed all such warnings, we become timid and blocked. Your goal as a creativity self-coach is neither to routinely ignore nor to routinely heed anxious warning signals but, through awareness and practice, sensibly deal with your anxious feelings case by case.

EXERCISE 17

Growing Your Anxiety Awareness

An anxiety expert is aware when he is anxious, understands the underlying causes of his anxiety, chooses whether or not to heed the warning, and knows what to do when he decides not to heed it. The first vital step in this four-step process is gaining anxiety awareness. As I mentioned previously, we are more likely to defend ourselves against an awareness of our anxiety than to frankly acknowledge that we are feeling anxious. We do this primarily by linguistic trickery, telling ourselves that we are tired, bored, confused, restless, depressed, unwell, and so on, when in fact we are anxious.

Only you can crack through your defensiveness and bravely acknowledge the presence of anxiety in your life. If you are interested in tackling this issue and becoming an anxiety expert, start by keeping an anxiety awareness journal. Carry it with you at all times and turn an inquisitive eye on your reactions to the situations that arise daily, whether it's deciding whether or not to jaywalk or deciding whether or not to continue writing your novel. Begin to recognize how anxiety manifests itself in your body — for instance, more as mental confusion, more as physical symptoms, or more as cognitive distortion — and what situations seem to regularly provoke anxiety.

You might find entries in your anxiety awareness journal that read like the following: "Skipped buying cereal at the supermarket today because it made me too anxious to choose between the cornflakes and the raisin bran. I started to get an actual upset stomach and still wasn't feeling all that well when I got home. Amazing! Who knew that such 'simple choices' could cause real anxiety? Imagine how much more anxiety I'll provoke tomorrow when I try to decide between sending Martha to Corsica or to Crete in chapter 2." Keep this journal for a month and start to become a real anxiety expert.

A creativity self-coach is obliged to become an anxiety expert by mastering the four steps outlined above and by going a step further and understanding the place of anxiety in the creative process. Why, to take one example, might nearing the end of writing your novel make you anxious? For several plain reasons which most writers choose not to notice: that soon you will have to read your novel and see if it is good or bad; that soon you will have to write a novel synopsis, a task that most writers find odious; that soon you will have to begin contacting agents and editors; that soon you will have to leave your characters behind, characters whom you may have grown to love; and that soon you will have to begin thinking about your next novel and starting the process (with its attendant anxiety) all over again.

None of this is mysterious. None of this is staggeringly hard to fathom. However, since we typically prefer not to think about these matters, we do not address the anxiety that wells up in us as we near the completion of our novel. We take a week off, we take a month off, we say things to ourselves like, "I just can't figure out how the damn thing ends!" In these and similar ways we avoid addressing our experience of anxiety. A writer who is also an anxiety expert recognizes that the prospect of completing her novel is making her anxious and sits herself down to address the matter as calmly and as forthrightly as she can.

Appreciating the Tao of Anxiety

Try the following four-step exercise. First, take a stab at articulating the stages of the creative process as you understand them. If you can't get a clear picture of the complete process or what stages you go through as you create, try at least to picture one part of the process — say, "starting to paint each day" or "completing a painting" or "showing my paintings to others."

Second, ask yourself, "What characteristically makes me anxious in each of these stages?" If you are looking at just one element of the process, reframe the question as (for example), "What characteristically makes me anxious as I near the completion of a painting?" Try to articulate both what makes you anxious and how that anxiety is manifested.

Third, try to answer the question, "What can I do to effectively deal with these regular, predictable experiences of anxiety?" Your answer might take the form of, "Just be aware that some anxiety is present and choose not to flee" or, "Have ready a deep-breathing technique that actually works to reduce my experience of anxiety."

Fourth, test out your answer the next time you experience anxiety during the creative process.

Eliminating anxiety is not an appropriate goal since anxiety alerts us to real threats as well as to conjured ones. You do, however, want to conjure fewer threats. The less you experience the opinions of others as a threat, the less you experience entering the unknown as a threat, the less you experience making creative choices as a threat, and so on, the less anxiety you will conjure and then have to manage. The anxiety that remains — that portion that neither will nor ought to go away — is yours to fathom and to handle brilliantly.

London, England

I have been working with a British journalist via email. He is good at his job, and his five-minute BBC radio pieces have won awards. He has spent the last ten years in far-flung places covering headline events and delivering quirky human-interest pieces. Now he is at London University on a prestigious fellowship, a fellowship available to only ten journalists annually. He applied for the fellowship because, as he indicated in his application, he craved the time and needed the financial support to write a book. He got the fellowship and now can't write.

He is making his wife crazy. One day he is enthusiastic about Book X and explains it to her at the breakfast table. She cries, "Go for it!" The next day he has abandoned Book X and is hot for Book Y. He describes it to her over toast and marmalade. "Go for it!" she cries. Day thirty-nine, when he comes down to breakfast with a new enthusiasm to breathlessly explain, she tells him, "Contact this creativity coach in America, or I will kill you."

He does. In the first week of email work I learn that he has ideas for seventy-three books, give or take a dozen. In the second week I learn that none of those seventy-three ideas really interests him. Most, he supposes, have been done already. Few have broad enough appeal to reach a mass audience. This one suffers from that flaw, and that one suffers from this flaw. This one might work, except for A, which could be cured by doing B, which raises the specter of C, which will surely cause D to happen, making it all unworkable.

He is faster than a speeding bullet as he grows tantalized by this idea, drops it, darts to that idea, makes it sound excellent, finds its flaw, and zooms away to something new. A second later he is back to the first idea, which is still problematic but which looks ever so much better since balloons two through ten have burst. It is all I can do not to throttle him across the reaches of cyberspace and just as hard not to send his wife an email of condolence.

Then, as it happens, I find myself in London. Andrew is living north of Hyde Park, and we make a date to meet in Hampstead, an upscale North London enclave of royals, psychiatrists, best-selling authors, and financiers. Dickens, Constable, Mondrian, H. G. Wells, D. H. Lawrence, Sting, and Boy George have all called Hampstead home. I've visited Hampstead four times before and once stayed for two months as part of a writing year abroad. I love it there.

It is the perfect place to wrestle face-to-face with Andrew's anxiety — for anxiety is surely the headline issue — since Hampstead is one of anxiety's true homes.

There, at 20 Maresfield Gardens, Freud landed after escaping Vienna in 1938. Now a museum, his home contains the iconic couch of psychoanalysis and his collection of toys, a collection so strange as to give one pause about his mental health. Hampstead is also home to the Anna Freud Centre, opened in 1940 by Freud's daughter as the Hampstead War Nursery providing foster care for Britain's orphans. The Centre is still going strong as a world-renowned child psychotherapy clinic.

I meet Andrew at an ancient pub just off the Hampstead high street. Tucked away on a narrow side street, the pub has substantial bench seating out front, and because it is a gorgeous sunny day, we choose to sit outside. Andrew is furtive. I wonder if his furtiveness is a calculated feature of his reporting persona, a result of his being coerced by his wife into seeing me, or proof that he is an anxious person. My nickel is on the last.

We exchange pleasantries and then get down to work. I want to experience his darting mind and generalized anxiety firsthand and say, "So, what book do you claim to be working on today?"

"Disputed islands!" he replies instantly. "Did you know that there are over 230 islands in the world that somebody is fighting over right now? The Spratly Islands between Hong Kong and Singapore, the Kurile Islands between Russia and Japan — "

"What would you want to say on the subject? What's interesting about these disputed islands?"

"I know! Probably they aren't interesting enough. I

think I'd rather do a book about the cult of beekeeping. There's so much new research on bees, and there's something especially weird and — almost spiritual — about the people who keep bees, who like to have their bodies covered by bees — "

I roll my eyes.

"You don't like that," he says. "I know. Small appeal. How about this one? 'Odd jobs in odd places.' There was this fellow I interviewed in Thailand who did healing rituals after sex-change operations. He took the male clothes you came in with and set them on fire, then he brought you this beautiful embroidered dress — "

"Stop!" I cry. The drinkers at the next bench glance up from their pints. "Somebody really wants to write that island book. Somebody really wants to write that bee book. You don't. Stop already with islands, bees, and burning pants!"

He looks away. I wait. At the tiny theater next door a man is changing posters. The new posters announce the world premiere of a play about a man's obsession with his cell phone. It is called *Mobile* and has, as its poster picture, the image of a man staring anxiously at his cell phone, waiting for it to ring. The teaser line is "His next call will change everything." Andrew speaks.

"I would like to do a book about what it is like to be thought of as gay when in fact you are not gay," he says. "In a working-class city in the north of England. I mean, that would be my story. But I would research it and get other stories. Maybe just men, maybe women too. But I think just men. A sort of nonfiction *Billy Elliott,* with,

I don't know — " He stops and looks away. "I suppose there are lots of problems with this idea — "

"Write this book," I say.

"What?"

"Write this book."

"Excuse me?"

"Write this book."

He looks at me. "I didn't know you would be direct. I expected some Freudian thing where you never voiced an opinion. You say that I should write this book?"

"I do. You've waited too long to write a book, and now you simply must write one. Good, bad, or indifferent. You've waited too long to test yourself, and the thought of testing yourself is making you so anxious that you can't commit to one idea for even a minute. Of all the ideas you've named, this one is the best. The richest. The truest. By a long shot. If you agree, that's that. That's the book you're writing. Do you agree?"

"I might."

"Do you agree?"

"Let's say that I do."

"Then that's that."

"What if — "

"Doesn't matter!"

"I could do it from a slightly different angle. I could — "

"No!"

"I need to research — "

"You need to write. You need to see if you have anything to say. You need to sit down and think about one thing for an hour straight, not for five seconds. You need to deal with the anxiety you feel, not let it send you flying off like an electron in a particle accelerator. You need to write about that boy and let the book idea grow as you write. You need to write."

"What if — "

"I don't want to hear it!" I put my fingers in my ears and start whistling. Andrew watches me. So do the four men at the next bench. "Yank," Andrew says. They nod knowingly.

"All right," Andrew says. "But I will have to go on the Web and do a little research. I feel I need to."

I relent. "One week of research. Then you start writing."

"All right."

"Now, how will you manage your anxiety?"

"My anxiety?"

"Your anxiety. Some would-be writers manage their anxiety by having no thoughts. They can't fail at writing a book if they banish all thoughts that might lead to a book. Not a very effective way to manage anxiety — but we aren't really very clever creatures. Some would-be writers — you, for instance — manage their anxiety by flitting from idea to idea. You will never have to write a bad book because you talk yourself out of every book idea within seconds of the idea surfacing. Also not very effective, because all you get from that maneuver is no book, disappointment, and depression. You have been managing the anxiety of perhaps writing a bad book ineffectively, and now we need to find you some effective ways of managing that anxiety."

"Like?"

"You tell me."

"Just being brave, I suppose. Being John Wayne. Did you know that apart from being scared to serve in the army he was probably gay — "

"There you go again! Talking about anxiety makes you anxious, and so you change the subject. This is your way. Changing the subject. This is your whole repertoire of dealing with anxiety. Changing the subject."

"I have no way of dealing with anxiety. Drugs?"

"Possibly."

"Or what?"

"Let me run through the list." I do just that. I name the handful of techniques proven effective in dealing with anxiety: the breathing techniques, the meditation techniques, the cognitive techniques, the discharge techniques. I model "silent screaming" and get another round of glances from the mates at the next bench. I talk Andrew through "one cleansing breath" and force him to try it. I finish with the headline that he has no choice but to practice and master one of these time-tested techniques or else invent one of his own. He agrees in a way that makes me doubt that he is agreeing.

It is time for us to end. I ask him a last question.

"What book are you working on?"

"Not a Faggot."

"Wow. Is that your working title?"

"It just came to me."

"Great! You mean to write it?"

"I suppose."

"That falls short of sounding like iron-willed determination."

"Well, I need to do the research first — "

"Of course!"

We gather our things, get to our feet, and shake hands. In the blink of an eye Andrew has darted away.

I go walking, stop at Keats's house, a lovely spot down a leafy side street, and sit on the front bench to write. I once wrote a good portion of a bad novel sitting on this bench, during my first stay in London. Blessed with arrogance, I presumed that the novel would be great. It wasn't. If I had revised it several times it surely would have been better — but I was too arrogant to revise. I had it so easy, after all, all the unrealized novels I wrote notwithstanding, because I had no anxiety to manage. To that a person who is made anxious by the prospect of writing can only exclaim, "Damn his good luck!"

I leave Keats's house and wander Hampstead Heath, an eight-hundred-acre tame wilderness of dark trails and duck ponds. I trudge up Parliament Hill, London's highest point, and at the summit picture a young Andrew coming to such a place to lick his wounds. What was his real story? I seriously doubted that he would manage to tell it. Writing made him too anxious, damn his bad luck. Life made him too anxious. To quell his experience of anxiety, all that he knew how to do was change the subject. I expected that he would. His best hope for a creative life was to own his anxiety rather than ignoring it, and by owning it to begin the process of mastering it. All I could do was cross my fingers.

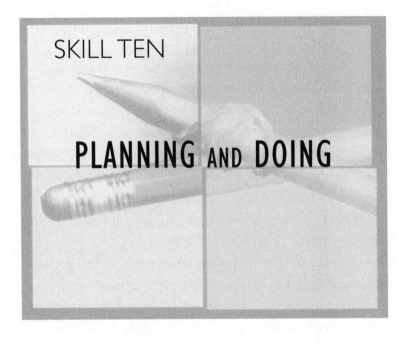

SKILL TEN

PLANNING AND DOING

Y ou have decided that you must paint abstract
landscapes, write a series of novels about psychological life in the suburbs, make a movie
about greed, compose for the violin, or investigate a certain
corner of theoretical physics. At some point you must actually do the thing you say you should be doing, rather than
wishing that you were doing it or making excuses for not
doing it. You must bite the bullet and do it, even if that
means making mistakes, falling short, and hurting your
heart in the process. You will not fail at writing a good
novel or making a good movie if you do no writing or

moviemaking, except that in the larger sense, you will have failed utterly.

When you accept that you must act — that it is time to act, that it is your responsibility to act, that you have no choice but to act — it is wise to make a plan. However, since we make so many resolutions and break them, set so many goals and fall short of realizing them, and create so many plans without following through on them, we become reluctant to plan. We prefer not to plan so as not to disappoint ourselves one more time. Burdened by the memory of the many times that we didn't follow through on our plan for losing weight, exercising, learning a new language, learning a new instrument, getting out of our small town, studying art instead of accounting, and so on, we find it too painful to sit down and make a plan for writing our novel or making our film. The mere thought of planning brings up feelings of shame, regret, and disappointment.

This is exactly why planning is so important. Those feelings of shame, regret, and disappointment are blockers that prevent us from taking action. We must overcome them, transcend them, move past them, and argue ourselves into an affirmative, life-loving stance. We must say something like, "Yes, I'm afraid, yes, I'm ashamed that I haven't done more already, yes, I'm sad that I've failed so many times, yes, I'm disappointed in myself that I took so many wrong turns, yes, I'm furious with the world for not supporting me better, yes, it feels ridiculous to start my novel for the hundredth time, having cavalierly abandoned

it ninety-nine times already, but now I will let go of all that
— *all* that! — and plan for the writing of my novel."

Agreeing to Plan

Have a heartfelt conversation with yourself about your
willingness or unwillingness to plan. You might start by
bravely acknowledging the many plans you created but
never followed, the many resolutions you broke, the many
dreams you deferred, the many goals you never achieved.
This examination will take a lot of courage and may produce a few tears. It's a liberating chat, though, and a way
to move past the past. Chat with yourself until you feel a
real willingness to plan. Try not to read on until you arrive
at that internal willingness.

Since you most likely have a negative history with planning, it will help if this time you follow these five golden
rules:

1. *Let the plan for your current project be simple.*
   It is hard enough to make a plan and keep to
   it. Adding details, rules, subideas, and com-
   plexities only makes this hard thing harder. A
   simple writing plan is to try to write every
   day. You can add this many minutes or that

many words to this plan as an added goal, but that added goal is also an added demand and may prove burdensome. "I intend to write every day" (or "I intend to paint every day," "I intend to compose every day," and so on) is about as perfect as a plan can get.

2. *Create a flexible long-term plan.* In addition to announcing a simple plan for your current project, a plan that might sound like "I will write every day," construct a long-term plan based on your mission statement and your vision of the tasks, milestones, and contours of your creative journey. This plan should contain markers that will help you know that you are on track, like, "I intend to have three short stories published in the next eighteen months" or, "I intend to have enough paintings for a show by the end of the year."

3. *Let your long-term plan be sensible.* Can you earn a living by writing short stories? Almost certainly not. Even though creating a plan is a moment of optimism as you recommit to your current creative project and rekindle your passion for creating, it is not a moment to engage in wishful thinking. Talk yourself out of plans that, on reflection, do not seem real enough. This internal conversation might sound like the following: "I'm aware that a couple of short story collections did very well in the marketplace, and I am very glad that they did,

since that gives me hope. But I don't think I
should draw the conclusion that I might be
able to make a living by writing short stories.
My better plan is to write excellent short stories, do my damnedest to get them published,
make a name for myself, and create a writing
life that works for me, which may include a
day job and which I will not judge on the
basis of my income from short story writing."

4. *Let the plan fit you.* I think it's a great idea to
do a good portion of your creative work first
thing in the morning, before your regular day
begins and before your brain cells get enlisted
for ordinary tasks. I try to sell this idea to every
client. But if you are certain that you work best
in the evening and that morning creating is out
of the question, then plan for evening creating.
You are your own self-coach, and you are the
one obliged to direct yourself wisely and well.
Just be honest with yourself and make plans
that are true to your best understanding of what
will really work for you.

5. *Revisit your plans frequently.* Bravely monitor
your plans regularly, as often as weekly in the
beginning. One day a week truthfully answer
the following two questions: "Have I been
keeping to my everyday plan?" and, "Have I
been keeping to my long-term plan?" If you
haven't, recommit to your creative life and

pledge to do a better job of following through.
If your plans ought to be changed, change
them. If they ought to be better honored as
they are, do a finer job of honoring them.

In responding to a training lesson on planning, Lucy, a
writer and coach-in-training, explained:

Even just thinking about planning has brought up
fears for me in the past: fear of being forced to do
something I haven't chosen myself, fear of failing
to do the plan at all or less than effectively, fear that
the plan isn't the right plan. Planning brings out my
inner critic who wants to judge whether I've lived
up to the plan. When this judge appears, I often
end up feeling depressed and guilty for "not doing
it good enough." What has worked best for me is to
find ways to make that inner voice my ally: to dialogue with it, update it on my current goals, get it
to agree to a less harsh way of evaluating, and be
more fluid in coming up with alternative ways to
accomplish something.

The deepest fear about making plans is about
taking action, period: that it won't be the "right"
action. I've spent years not acting on what has the
deepest meaning for me, for fear that I might not
make the right choice. What has helped me is to
remember that not taking action is like killing my
creative self and that accepting being creative means

making mistakes and messes. Affirming these things has helped me in my creative process, and also helped me feel more at ease in suggesting plans to clients and reassuring them that setting a plan doesn't mean setting themselves up for failure.

Now that I'm getting used to making plans for creative projects, I'm pleasantly surprised to see some of its positive aspects. I'm finding that making a plan for writing creates a better connection between me and the project, an alliance of sorts, that is firmer than if I just "think about" the project in a general way. The plan creates a place for the writing to be held and take shape, the way a pottery jar holds grain. I still keep an eye on the plan so that it doesn't become too rigid a container — the pottery jar is made of a clay that never dries and I can keep reshaping it as needed.

EXERCISE 20

Creating Your Everyday Plan
and Your Long-Term Plan

Create a breathtakingly simple everyday plan and a robust, detailed, marker-filled long-term plan. The first might come in at five or six words; the second might run to two full pages.

You have a simple, brilliant everyday plan in place, a plan that sounds like "I will write every day." Today dawns. You know that your entire task is just to start, to get to the computer, to get your computer booted up, to get the file containing your current writing open, to begin. Somehow, you can't. Maybe what's stopping you is fear. Maybe it's anxiety. Maybe you feel overwhelmed by the number of things you have to do. Maybe you're so worried about your current situation that you can't concentrate. Maybe your heart has been wounded too many times by rejection. Whatever it is that is blocking you, *something* is. It is real, palpable, as solid as a brick wall. You have your brilliant plan, but you can't get from where you are to your computer. What can you do?

If a self-coach can answer no other question, she must be able to answer this one. What will you do when you can't create, when, to use the word that we have become accustomed to using, you *block?* I've presented many answers already: you could use the Centering Sequence or some other centering tactic, you could use one of your anxiety management tools — say, a guided visualization or an affirmation, you could remind yourself of your mission statement and talk yourself into passionately making meaning, and so on. You could try these and a hundred other tactics. I suspect you think that now I am going to say, "But what you really should do is X." *There is no X!*

Would-be creators and blocked creators dream about magical cures. There are none. There are only small, real, honest things to try. If the inner compulsion to create were powerfully present, if you were obsessed, passionate, and dying to write, you would be flying to your computer. You would be like the thirsty man who sees the oasis in the distance and starts running. If you are blocked, this isn't you. You are thirsty, there is the oasis, and you stand stock-still, prevented by powerful forces from doing the natural thing, taking one step and then another step and arriving at the water. If, in your paralysis, you say to yourself, "I'll wait for the magic carpet ride," you will die of thirst. What you must say to yourself is, "One step, then another." If you can take those first steps, you may find yourself running.

Make plans and train yourself to honor them.

Fort Worth, Texas

I couldn't stop thinking about barbecue. I was in Fort Worth to present a workshop at the annual conference of the United States Institute of Theater Technology, the organization that is home to costume designers, lighting directors, stage managers, and other "backstage" theater professionals, and noticed in the program that on the conference's last day the organizers were hosting the "world's biggest barbecue" on the convention center floor. There would be chicken stations, rib stations, hot link stations, shredded beef stations. To a Jew from Brooklyn able to eat a whole corned beef or pastrami by the time I was eight, with nothing but celery soda and maybe a sour pickle for accompaniment, this was a vision of paradise. It made you proud to be an American.

I had been invited to speak by the costume design division of the Institute and had my first barbecue of the week with a group of costume designers at a small Fort Worth barbecue joint. The designers knew me from a column I was writing in those days for *Callboard* magazine called "Staying Sane in the Theater." It was a question-and-answer column, and for the first few months of the column's existence I'd had to make up the questions to answer. Then one day a letter came in, from an actor hospitalized because of an acute psychotic episode, containing a year's worth of excellent questions. I spent the next year answering that poor fellow's questions, each month changing his initials.

This first foray into Fort Worth barbecue was sadly disappointing, since the ribs seemed quite ordinary, but we had a fine time chatting about the issues faced by behind-the-scenes theater people, issues not so different from those faced by most people in the arts. There were the chronic, repetitive periods of unemployment between gigs; the crazy-making challenges that big egos, sparse resources, and tight schedules produced; the unfortunate but mandatory catering to a public that preferred revivals to experiments; the financial woes of local theaters everywhere. We laughed, drank, and picked our dry ribs clean.

After lunch we returned to the convention center for an afternoon of workshops. I wasn't presenting until the next day and planned to sit in on some of them. I find the workshops at conferences where I'm presenting fascinating, and I have made it a habit of sitting in on them. I particularly like the annual Romance Writers of America conference where, for instance, you can attend a whole workshop on when to give your editor a half-pound of Godiva chocolates and when to splurge on a full pound. But here the workshops had names like "Electricity 101," "Hands-on WYSWIG," "Can You Read and Speak MSDS?" and "Monster Makeup." I decided to pass.

I found a corner sofa near the coffee cart and prepared to do a little writing.

"Eric?"

I looked up, saw a woman about my age, and got to my feet. She extended her hand, and I shook it.

"I'm Helga. We met in Iceland many years ago. I saw you listed in the program and wondered if we'd run into each other."

It all came rushing back to me. We had been much younger then, twenty-five years younger. I had come to Eastern Iceland to visit a friend who was teaching English at a boarding school there. I flew by small plane from Reykjavík to the airport in Egilsstadir, Eastern Iceland's largest town, which then had a population of six hundred and has since swollen to twelve hundred. I was picked up at the airport — airstrip, really — by a young, garrulous fellow and whisked by jeep over rutted roads through a lunar landscape — the astronauts use Iceland to simulate the moon — to the boarding school, nestled beneath the eastern edge of a thousand-mile-long glacier.

It was late in the evening, but the school was alive with activity. It turned out that I had arrived just in time for the annual Edda Pageant, a performance the boarding students put on to celebrate Icelandic culture and the great poetic *eddas,* also known as sagas, that are filled with some of the strongest women that legend and literature have ever produced. The students were performing excerpts from sagas with names like *Cormac's Saga, Grettir's Saga,* and the *Saga of Burnt Njal,* operatic, swashbuckling sagas that, being in Icelandic, could not quite keep me awake.

Exhausted, I trudged off to my room and fell asleep, only to be awakened several hours later by a grand commotion and hundreds of flashlight beams cutting the night. My friend rushed in to get a warmer jacket and stopped long enough to tell me what was happening. A teacher — it turned out to be Helga — had left a note saying that she was committing suicide by walking off into the glacial darkness to freeze to death. Everyone knew what was going on: Helga's husband, Jon, had started having an affair with another teacher at the school. Helga couldn't stand it, the humiliation, primarily, and had taken off to die. The whole school was out with flashlights looking for her.

I tossed and turned but still managed to sleep. The next day dawned eerily quiet. I learned that Helga had been found and that she was physically all right. A few days later I was out walking by the river that flowed out of the glaciers, a river made white by glacial runoff, and ran into Helga. I knew her by sight, and she knew me as the visiting American. We talked, though not about her recent difficulties. At that time I was working on a novel, and I told her about it.

"You write every day?" she asked.

"I try."

"I drink every day."

"There's that."

"My brother in Reykjavík calls himself a writer, but he never writes."

I nodded.

"He does manage to drink every day," she continued wryly.

"There you go."

"What allows you to do that? To write every day?"

"I just wake up wanting to write."

"Do you have any idea how lucky you are?"

"Probably not."

The next day we met again. Was it by accident? We ended up talking about the tonal differences between the words *goal* and *plan*. I thought that *goal* was a beautiful, lofty word but needed its partner, *plan,* an ordinary, even boring word, to support it and breathe life into it. I said something clever like "a goal without a plan is like a Rolls Royce without wheels." I had recently graduated with an undergraduate degree in philosophy and was in the habit of talking that way.

I didn't see Helga again. I heard that she had left Jon and the school and flown off to Reykjavík. Now she filled me in on the intervening twenty-five years. What followed were two or three bad years of too much alcohol and too much despair. Then, quite by accident, a friend invited her to come to Copenhagen and help on a play for which he was in charge of the lighting. She discovered that she loved stage lighting. She worked in Europe for several years, then was invited to New York, where she was given chief lighting duties on one Broadway play after another. Now she was quite the star. If you wanted your play spectacularly lit, you wanted Helga.

"That was quite a journey," I said.

"You and I had a conversation by the river about goals and plans. Do you remember that? We decided that *goal* was sexier and more exciting and that *plan* was dowdy and boring. But there was much more muscle in a sentence like 'I plan to write every day' than in a sentence like 'My goal is to write every day.' It was like the difference between getting up and going to work or staying in bed wishing that the work would get done. I'd been spending a lot of time in bed entirely depressed and couldn't deal with 'goals.' But I could deal with a daily plan."

"That conversation by the river changed my life," Helga continued. "I needed something simple but not stupid to anchor me in that crazy time, and I said to myself, 'I will make a daily plan first thing each morning and see how that goes.' My first plan was 'get to Reykjavík.' That was easy. When it got harder I stopped planning. I was a mess and couldn't keep to anything. But I did keep holding the sanctity of the word *plan*. I held its sanctity without actually being able to plan. Then, in Copenhagen, lighting that first show, it fell into place.

"It became my meditation practice, making that daily plan. I would sit with my cup of coffee and grow quiet as I thought about what my day could include. There's a line by Gropius that I love: 'Only work which is the product of inner compulsion can have spiritual meaning.' When I was teaching at that school, I had no inner compulsion to create. I wanted to create, but that isn't the same thing. My life was organized around Jon, teaching, being dutiful, getting things done. When he started his affair everything fell apart because I had never fallen in love with any art. Remember that we talked about you writing every day? Obviously you had that inner compulsion. I didn't then.

"But when I discovered stage lighting, I fell in love. I had always loved light, but I hadn't wanted to become a photographer or a painter. I had no container for my love of light. Then came the stage and the drama of lighting a stage. I fell in love and began to wake up every morning with an inner compulsion to light the play that I was currently working on. I wanted to comprehend everything about stage lighting. Daily planning fit like a glove. I had the goal, to be lighting director on great plays, and the habit of planning.

"Probably I don't need to plan my days anymore. Probably I plan automatically now. I could just get up and follow the routine I know so well. But I wouldn't dream of giving up that planning ritual! It's like a beautiful picture I draw for myself, my 'plan for the day.' It always includes a treat — for instance, I love good licorice. And it always includes substantial work, something where I can go deep, if only for an hour. There are days where everything could be just drudgery, an acrimonious meeting, a piece of equipment that isn't working, another change the director suddenly throws at me, and so on. But my daily plan takes all that into account by allocating some sacred spaces, for licorice and also for good work, like the lighting texts I love to write. Well. Our two talks by the river were lucky for me."

"What's your plan for the rest of the afternoon?"

"At four I give the main address for the lighting division. Did I forget to tell you that I am a star in my own small pond?" She laughed. "Then I have to fly back to New York for a planning meeting on my next play, a Broadway revival of Ibsen. I am so curious about how to light Ibsen! I want to sell the director on certain ideas, and I will be planning my line of attack with him on the plane ride back."

"Too bad," I said. "You'll be missing what's billed as the world's largest barbecue. It happens on the convention floor the last evening of the conference."

"I'm a vegetarian," she said. "I would have skipped that anyway. That would not have been in my plans."

We laughed, got to our feet, and shook hands warmly. Helga turned and hurried off. Her heels clacked on the convention floor. I watched her disappear. I shook my head, sat down to write, and found that I couldn't. Instead I began to dream, not of rib stations and chicken stations but of glacial rivers and lunar landscapes.

UPHOLDING DREAMS
AND TESTING REALITY

We must dream large, and we must also reality-test well. It is imperative that we do both. A person who dreams large but doesn't effectively test reality ends up living in a fantasy world. A person who tests reality well but doesn't nurture large dreams lives paralyzed in the ordinary world. A person who manages to do both occupies the only heaven heavenly enough to suit our creative soul, a heaven where creative projects are incubated and made manifest in the crucible of reality.

A symphony is conjured, composed, and performed. A novel is imagined, sweated out, and sanctified by purchasing librarians. A painting is envisioned, created, and honored in some museum or family home. This is our heaven. First comes the dream, the desire, the inner compulsion, the passion, the obsession. Next comes the testing in the real world, the sweat, the phone calls, the revisions, the disappointments, the commitment to more effort. The dream is the helium balloon, and reality is the string. A wise creator joyously fills up his balloon but keeps the string firmly in his grasp.

Many people live in a fantasy world of all-dream, no-reality. Year after year they people their unwritten screenplay with the hottest actors, find their unwritten poetry superior to all poetry extant, mentally patent and make millions from their untested inventions. Or they actually write their screenplay but market it by sending form postcards to world-famous directors, write their poetry but submit it to reviews that haven't published poetry in two decades, build and test their widget and then wait by the phone for a call from an investment banker. This is not good.

Even more people live in the ordinary world of all-reality, no-dream. Maybe they once had a dream. Maybe that dream still burns fiercely within them but more as pain than as passion. Maybe they never had permission to dream. Life is now made up of work, more work, a little pleasure, more work, errands, crises, and more work. They can plan, but not in service of their soul. They sometimes succeed, but not at what they love. This, too, is not good.

The very act of creating is a confrontation between

dream and reality, a marriage of dream and reality, a soaring melody moored by the mathematics of music, a fantastic journey anchored in the psychological makeup of its characters, a sculpture rooted to the ground by the perfection of anatomy. Every creator is dreaming but using the actual stuff of life, the formulas of chemistry, the lightness of feathers, the pliability of clay. Without a dream, the clay just sits there. Without the clay, the imagined jar holds no water.

In his essay "Create Dangerously" Albert Camus explained, "The loftiest work will always be the work that maintains an equilibrium between reality and man's rejection of reality, each forcing the other upward in a ceaseless overflowing, characteristic of life itself at its most joyous and heart-rending. Then, every once in a while, a new world appears, different from everyday reality and yet the same, full of innocent insecurity, called forth for a few hours by the power and longing of genius" (*Resistance, Rebellion, and Death,* trans. Justin O'Brien [New York: Vintage Books, 1995]). The dreamer rejects reality, the realist rejects the dream, the artist embraces both dream and reality.

In your art and in your creative life, you uphold the dream and you respect reality. On a day that is too real, you remind yourself, "I have a dream!" On a day that is too idle, you remind yourself, "Get real!" Your meaning-making mission is predicated on principles that you deem worthy — principles like witnessing for the culture, providing beauty, moving thought forward — and, since dreaming and reality-testing are both needed to fulfill your mission, both are moral imperatives. Both belong in a principled life.

Dancing the Dream-It, Do-It Dance

Done much dancing lately? Clear a nice space in your living room or kitchen. Put on some dance music. Dance up a storm while singing the following lyric: "I dream. I reality-test. I dream. I reality-test. I don't do just one. I don't do just the other. I dream. I reality-test. I dream. I reality-test. I don't do just one. I don't do just the other. Cha-cha-cha." Make up some more verses. Get someone to dance with you. Invite your friends over and start a conga line. Dance till you drop.

As a less fanciful and outrageous (but also less dramatic and energetic) exercise, answer the following three questions for yourself: "Do I keep dream-upholding and reality-testing in good balance? Do I incline one way or the other? If I incline this way or that, what ought I to do to regain and maintain a good equilibrium?"

What if reality has crushed your dream? This is likely to be the central problem you will face as a creativity self-coach, the problem that trumps all other problems. There is just too much reality. It grinds fine, it grinds mercilessly, it grinds until the end of time. If you are caught in the vise-grip of reality and can't find the wherewithal to sustain your dream, what can you do? Belinda, a creativity coach I trained, found herself in this situation with a despairing client:

> I have a client who has experienced so many disappointments in her life that she hardly dares to dream anymore. When I invited her to tell me what held energy or passion for her, she replied, "Nothing!" When I probed further, I was relieved to find that she could remember a dream she held before she lost hope. But when she expressed it, the dream came out so large that she saw it as impossible to accomplish. Her own inner reality-testing scanned the dream, saw it as impossible, and scratched it right off. She could say what her dream was but couldn't believe in it and therefore rejected it right away.
>
> In the face of her feelings of hopelessness, I found that I had to reach deep down inside myself for the courage to suggest that she take some small action in support of her dream. After I took a deep breath and searched for hope to extend to this client, I was surprised to hear back from her that she could see the value in trying for just a portion of her dream. It turns out that she is willing to take small steps and aim for bite-sized goals. She still gets depressed about how little she accomplishes, but she seems to be willing to accomplish her dream a little bit at a time.

EXERCISE 22
Upholding the Dream

You have a dream. Maybe it is to write and publish an excellent novel. You dare not say it, but you hope that your novel will transform the world a little and move people in the direction you feel they ought to move. Good for you! If no one held that dream, what kind of place would this be? Probably you also dream that your novel will bring you fame, glory, riches, great sex, and a step closer to a Nobel Prize. No doubt your ego is involved in the equation. Nothing wrong with that! Your dream is fine, righteous, and worthy.

Reality, however, has probably dented your dream a bit. Therefore the question is, "What will you do to uphold your dream?" It is so important to arrive at good answers to this question that you may want to keep a journal devoted to nothing but dream-upholding. Begin by announcing, "My dream is..." Every day, write a little, just a sentence or two, maybe a paragraph at most, on how you will uphold your dream that day. Use this journal to create disappointment exorcisms, pain relievers, and dream affirmations.

There is something absurd about dreaming, just as there is something absurd in the idea of passionately making meaning. It feels absurd to take life as seriously as it demands to be taken. But it also feels absurd to take life anything less than seriously, since the path of self-dismissal and self-disparagement can also be experienced as absurd. It feels absurd to say that you are free, given all life's constraints, and absurd to say that you are not free, given that you have plays you could write or sonatas you could compose. The playwright Eugéne Ionesco eloquently described living in the grip of this painful absurdity:

> Which is the right way? Indifference, perhaps. That's not possible; since we are here, we can't help participating. We cannot reject the world. Then let's take everything seriously; that's equally ridiculous. Or can I be like a tree? But I'm not a tree. Or can I follow the drift of history in the direction of cosmic evolution? But nobody knows quite what that means. One ought at least to feel at ease. I cannot, because living is the source of my unease. I seem to be going around in a circle. Perhaps I'm not going around in a circle. Perhaps there is no circle. I cannot laugh, nor weep, nor sit down, nor get up, nor desire, nor not desire. I am paralyzed. (*Fragments of a Journal,* trans. Jean Stewart [New York: Grove Press, 1968])

I ask the creativity coaches I train to think about these matters. Leslie, a coach-in-training, responded:

> I'm back from a long weekend in Canada for Thanksgiving. These questions resonated through

the trip and through family conversations. No one else in the extended family is an artist or writer or attempting to be one, but each person had a dream and in some way each of these dreams was "absurd." I don't know if my sister-in-law can open her own spa, but that is her dream. I don't know if my mother-in-law can live independently anymore, but that absolutely is her dream. Can my step-daughter have her own yoga studio, even though she knows zip about bookkeeping and insurance? Ya know what? I don't know.

Maybe this is the coaching middle ground of simultaneously trying to reality-test and dream-uphold with clients: I do know some of the questions to ask. I ask my mother-in-law, "What does your doctor say?" And, "Can you afford a nurse?" I ask my sister-in-law, "Have you ever worked in a spa?" And, "Might someone take you on as an apprentice?" I ask my stepdaughter, "Do you know what QuickBooks is?" And, "Is there studio space to rent in your town?" Each dream will demand answers to questions like these, and I suspect that reality will do enough hole-punching that I don't have to punch holes, too. I can just ask straightfor-ward questions, out of kindness and love, and try to be of help.

If your dream is to create deeply, to create well, and to create often, you already know how hard it is to keep your dream afloat. On Monday your mind punches a hole in your dream by announcing that you're too busy to create. On Tuesday your mate punches a hole in your dream by reminding you that you're further in debt. On Wednesday your culture punches a hole in your dream by hyping a best-selling book, a blockbuster film, or a monster album, flooding you with envy. On Thursday your parents punch a hole in your dream by innocently remarking how talented your brother is. On Friday a literary agent or gallery owner punches a hole in your dream by saying nothing whatsoever. How long is it before your dream sinks completely out of sight?

Reach down with both hands and pull your drowning dream back out of the water. Put it on a high-and-dry pedestal and polish it every day with good will and a dose of reality — don't forget that dose of reality. Otherwise your dream will not shine. A certain kind of heroism, needed to keep your dream afloat, is wonderful but not enough. A dual heroism is required, of courageous dream-upholding and courageous reality-testing.

Berkeley, California

I am presenting an afternoon workshop to the Berkeley chapter of the California Writers Club. The group meets monthly in a side room of a Mexican restaurant distinguished from similar Mexican restaurants by a glass-enclosed booth in the middle of the main dining room where you can watch your tortilla chips being baked. I arrive early and observe this chip-making process as writers gather nervously for the workshop.

They are more nervous than eager because mine is a role-playing workshop in which volunteers will come forward to pitch their current writing project. They will pitch it to a fellow writer playing the role of literary agent or book editor. These writers have read about my workshop in their monthly newsletter, and probably attendance will be down. Already the theme for the workshop — high anxiety — is apparent as twenty writers gather reluctantly and laugh anxiously.

I make my appearance. We settle, and I am introduced. It is time for me to insist that they bite the bullet. I get to my feet.

"You have a dream," I tell them. "You want to have your book published. The reality is that you must pitch your book in order to sell it. You pitch it through query letters, book proposals, and other written documents, and you also sometimes pitch it live when you meet an agent or an editor at a writer's conference or a book event. We are going to role-play those interactions.

"Why role-play, you ask? For several reasons. Because you need the practice. Because you never see these private moments between writers and agents and editors. Because your only experience of them is when you pitch your own work, which happens rarely and which probably makes you so anxious that you have little idea of what transpired.

"There are other good reasons, too. Learning to talk calmly and intelligently about your book helps you better understand what it is about — and what it isn't about — and makes revising it that much easier. You'll also do more writing if you feel comfortable that you can pitch what you write. The last reason is that we do such a terrible job of describing our own work! Our pride, our anxiety, our lack of preparation, our investment in the outcome get in the way and cause us to forget even the name of our own novel.

"That's where this workshop comes in. Here you'll get to see pitches and, if you bravely volunteer, practice your own pitch. All right? Let's begin! We need somebody to play a literary agent, the ruder and more insulting the better [this gets a nervous, conspiratorial laugh], and someone to come forward to pitch his or her latest project."

No one moves. Long seconds pass. At ten seconds I say, "Excellent! This is the most important lesson you'll learn this afternoon. Can you feel the anxiety in the room? Great! This is the anxiety you must deal with." I pause. "Who wants to play the agent?"

Five more seconds pass. Finally someone at a back table exclaims, "Oh, all right, if you really need an agent!" She comes forward to a round of applause and sits down in one of the two facing chairs in front of me.

"Now, who wants to be the writer?"

No one moves. Ten seconds pass. To the twenty writers in attendance, it must feel like days. Finally, at fifteen or twenty seconds, a woman says, "Well, I don't want to come up!" and gets up.

She comes forward to a round of relieved and grateful applause. She seats herself in the chair facing the "agent."

Both writers laugh nervously. As they await my instructions they make lame jokes and squirm uncomfortably.

I turn to the agent and say, "Begin." The writer playing the agent makes a face and replies, "I have no idea what to ask." I say, "Of course you do," and wait. She shakes her head, makes another lame joke, and then solicits the audience for suggestions. I tell them not to help. Finally she settles into her role and wills herself to understand what an agent might ask. A question comes to her.

"What's your book about?" she says.

I give her a round of facetious applause. She responds with a facetious bow.

Now it is the writer's turn to act as if she has no idea what to say. She makes faces, starts sentences, stops them. Finally she opts for an ironic approach. "I couldn't possibly tell you in just a couple of words," she says. "Let me send you the whole manuscript."

The audience laughs. I chide them. "No! This is the work. She must find a way to present her book. It may take her three attempts, it may take her thirty attempts. But this is the work." I turn to the writer. "Try again."

She describes her book. No one can follow her confused description. I tell her to try again. She opts for a different approach. This one befuddles us even more. I make her try again. She does — and at last we come to understand that her book is a novel set in the 1890s. How long it has taken her to tell us even the simplest thing! I make her stop and start fresh several more times. Finally — finally! — she clearly presents her work. "It's a historical novel," she says, "based on a true story of love and cannibalism in the backwoods of Montana. The main characters are Montana's first Buddhist monk and the granddaughter of Abraham Lincoln."

The room erupts with applause.

To save a little time I say, "What else might this agent ask her? Just the most obvious questions. What have you written before? Who's seen the manuscript so far? Who do you see as the audience for your book? How much of it is done? How long is the manuscript? What will you do to support your book when it comes out? For each of these questions you want to prepare a useful, sensible answer. To the question, 'What have you written before,' you don't answer, 'Well, I guess you saw right through me!' To the question, 'How long is your novel,' you don't reply, 'It's pretty fat and could use some trimming.' To the question, 'Who's seen it so far,' you don't respond, 'A few of my friends, some of whom kind of liked it.'" I turn to the agent. "Try this question on her: 'Who do you see as the audience for your book?'"

The agent asks the writer my question. The writer thinks. She doesn't squirm, act out, or stubbornly resist. She thinks. We see her prepare and reject answers, phrase and rephrase her response. She is no longer a supplicant or a combatant but a writer trying to prepare a good answer. Finally she speaks.

"I see as my audience the same people who loved Fanny Mae Smith's excellent *My Brother, My Butcher* and Rita Jo Coolidge's *When Love Comes for Dinner.* Readers with Eastern leanings will be interested in the story because one of the characters is a Buddhist monk, and people who love Lincoln will be fascinated to hear what happened to one of his granddaughters."

The room is thrilled. "Great!" I exclaim. I turn to the agent. "Give her what she wants. Say, 'I think I'd like to look at your synopsis and the first fifty pages of your novel. Do you have any questions?'"

The agent repeats my words. I turn to the writer. "First, give her a really inappropriate answer."

The writer thinks. Suddenly she laughs, snaps her fingers, and turns to the agent. "Oh, really? I don't have a synopsis — does that matter? Personally, I think that synopses are stupid. I mean, what justice can a synopsis do to a novel? And what do you charge? — 15 percent? Isn't that a lot? Can't you make it 10 percent for me, since I'm a poor, starving writer? And when will I hear back from you? What — in four to six weeks? That's much too long! Can't you get back to me in a week? Naturally I'm in a rush to get this published."

The writers stomp their feet. Of course they want to talk this way to agents.

"Now give her the right answer," I say.

The writer takes a deep breath. "No, I don't have any questions. I look forward to talking with you after you've had a chance to look at my materials. Thank you!"

Is getting this right so hard? Emotionally speaking, it appears to be. Every silly, stubborn, resentful, prideful, self-sabotaging bone in our body starts quivering in the presence of marketplace players. We react like a dancing skeleton on a string. Forced to admit that we have inchoate knowledge of our work and an unconvincing presentation, we want to lash out or run and hide rather than stay put and present ourselves better. I facilitate another two role-plays, and these Berkeley writers see the mischief repeat itself. However, they also see the role-players get more comfortable, more proficient, more real as they practice.

Writers hear over and over again that agents and editors are busy people, far too busy to put up with writers who can't or won't present themselves clearly and quickly. Writers hear these things a million times over, hating what they hear, but until they see these interactions role-played they tend not to get it. These writers get to see for themselves what editors and agents see all the time: nervous presentations that hurt the writer's case, responses that fail to grab the listener's attention, woefully inadequate answers to the simplest questions. They witness important things left unsaid, profound lapses of memory, endless missed opportunities. When the time comes, these twenty writers are very ready for a break.

On break, I think of a dear friend of mine. We met thirty years ago at San Francisco State University in the graduate creative writing program. We have been friends ever since, although for much of that time she has lived in Europe and we lost close touch. She has had a real life, including raising a child by herself and running various nonprofit organizations. Somehow she has upheld the writing dream for all these years, slowly but surely writing good novels, despite the fact that no agent or editor has ever taken an interest in her work.

Recently she completed a new novel. It is amazing that she still writes, amazing that her heart has held, amazing that hope still floats. She asked for my help in marketing the novel to agents, but like the writers here at the workshop, like the lion's share of creative people I have coached, her initial impulse was to balk at my suggestions. However, I wouldn't relent. It took me months — not minutes, not hours, not days, but months — to convince her that there were worse ways and better ways to approach agents and that she was taking the path of most resistance.

Finally — finally! — she listened.

Now an agent is excited to represent her. That is wonderful news. Why, though, did I have to go at her with a hammer and chisel to get her to do the most obvious things? What causes resistance so fierce that even a jackhammer can't dent it? I have been guilty of this same resistance a thousand times over and still succumb to it daily, harming myself by taking this pig-headed stand or that self-defeating shortcut. Why?

The break ends, and I return to my anxious writers. I am not armed with any new answers, but I feel a renewed desire to help them support their dreams in the crucible of reality. I see, when I return, that they have paired up and are courageously practicing their pitches.

SKILL TWELVE

MAINTAINING A CREATIVE LIFE

C ountless forces align on the side of not creating. You bravely write a novel; no publisher buys it; what do you do next? You paint; beauty eludes you; what do you do next? You sing but have doubts about your talent and fears about your future. One day a man you don't love says, "I can make your life easy." What do you do? You choose a scientific field; it bores you; but you are tenured. What do you do? The blocks, challenges, and temptations come like waves from the sea, one after another.

I could simply say, "Become the best damned creativity self-coach possible!" And I *am* saying that. What that implies, however, is that you become a practiced dreamer, a great realist, an anxiety expert, a true day laborer, a cognitive therapist, a dynamo, a master at stillness, a habitual planner, a holistic thinker. Can anyone measure up to this? I believe that you can. I think that you are ready for exactly this work.

You are ready for this work, and you will also resist it. When I coach a client, I don't doubt her intentions, but I also don't suppose that her human resistance to self-awareness and hard work will magically vanish. We possess as many blind spots as a potato has eyes and as many excuses as a politician has promises. I believe that you want to do the work I've outlined, and I also believe that you will have to make an almost superhuman effort to get this work accomplished.

Every day you will need to reflect on your life and chart your course. Every day you will have to renew the pact you made with yourself to act as if you matter. Every day you will need to forgive yourself and others to release your pent-up pain and disappointment. Every day you will need to surrender to the facts of existence while doing your damnedest to realize your dreams. Oh, there are some days when you can sit on the beach and work on your tan. But not many.

Every day you will need to dispute your human tendency to deal with creative blocks ineffectively. Every day you will need to seek out solitude, where you can create, and human contact, for warmth and love. Every day you will need to take some action — small, medium, or large

— in the service of your creative life. Yes, some days
can soak in the tub and eat chocolate. But not many.

Every day is an opportunity to have some success, even
if that success is just doing the righteous work that gets
you closer to the success that you crave. First and foremost, every day is a day to restore hope. Each time a little
hope returns, each time the flicker of a hopeful smile plays
across your lips, each time you feel desire well up in you
again, that is a day full of promise. Restoring hope may
sound like a strange daily task, but it is your most important one. Your self-coaching persona must get in the first
word each morning: "I have hope for this day."

You might even love these challenges. It is bound to feel
satisfying to put your talents to good use. It is sure to warm
your heart to know that you have done a creative day's work.
How much better will you sleep after coming home from your
day job and, instead of flipping on the television, turning to
your painting or your novel writing? You have tasks to perform every day, tasks assigned by your creativity self-coach,
and, who knows, it may even thrill you to perform them.

EXERCISE 23
Stocking Your Creativity Kit

Put a creativity kit together. Store the items on a conve-
nient shelf or in a handy box. Add additional items to the
kit as you see fit, for instance, ones that I've described in
previous chapters, like the anxiety awareness journal from
chapter 9, or ones that you dream up yourself.

Your creativity kit should include:

- *A project log.* Give each project (each short story, each painting, each song, each invention) several pages of its own in a log in which you keep a record of your projects' progress. Better yet, give each project its own small notebook, maybe a "blue book" of the sort that college students use to take essay exams.

- *A daily calendar.* Get or make a calendar that devotes a page to each day. Divide each day into two parts. Every morning, write down your daily goals with respect to your creative life and *only* your creative life. No "take the cat to the vet" or "renew car insurance" entries on this calendar. Your goals can be of the "I will write today" variety, or they can be more specific goals like "I will send out three query emails today" or "I will prepare three new canvases." Every evening, use the bottom half of the page to comment on the day, summarizing to what extent you achieved your goals.

- *A creativity to-do list pad.* Devote a to-do list pad to your creative projects and efforts. As with your daily calendar, do not put items on this list of the "clean the drapes" variety. This is not a daily list but an ongoing list that you never complete, on which you continually cross off items and continually add new ones. To repeat: this is not a list you complete, this is a way to organize and monitor your creative life.

- *Some meaningful objects or totems.* I keep certain postcards and photographs of Paris where I can see them, since they make me smile and support my creative efforts. I also keep a smooth pebble handy that I squeeze in conjunction with a ritual I use to strengthen my connection to my current work. Add objects and totems of this sort to your creativity organizer kit.

If you are interested in making meaning through creating, in manifesting your potential, in surviving the rigors of a creative life, and in managing the light and shadow of your contradictory personality, you must learn to become your own creativity self-coach. While you may sometimes hire a creativity coach and sometimes receive advice and counsel from other people, the main coaching you receive must come from you. Ultimately, there is only you.

What kinds of help does a top-flight athletic coach provide his athletes? All the following. You too can act as your own top-flight coach:

- He knows the game. He knows the rules, the traditions, the realities, the subtleties, the nuances of his sport. *Know your game.*

- She teaches. She teaches the fundamentals and building blocks of her sport, and more complex things like, in football, zone defenses and blitz packages. *Learn from real experience and teach yourself what you need to know.*

- He motivates. He cheerleads, cajoles, practices tough love, and is a master of psychology. *Motivate yourself. Psyche yourself up.*

- She is an unabashed advocate. She roots for her team, not the other team, and for her players, not the other players. *Get on your own side.*

- He is a dreamer and a realist, someone who dreams about winning championships but who knows when his team is only third- or fourth-best in the league (which, however, doesn't prevent him from trying to win a championship). *Never stop dreaming. Never stop being real.*

- She is a tactician and a strategist. If she is a baseball coach, she knows when to bunt and when to hit and run. If she is a tennis coach, she tells you when to play at the net and when to play at the baseline. *Own strategies for maneuvering the stages of the creative process and the tasks of a creative life.*

- He is a planner, scheduler, and prioritizer. He plans his pitching rotation so that none of his pitchers develops a sore arm; he organizes his practices so as to maximize the available time. *Plan — and follow through on your plans.*

- She is a compassionate witness. She tells players what she sees, not to hurt their feelings but to make them better players. *Monitor yourself with a compassionate but resolute third eye.*

- He hands over responsibility. His players must play the game, and he lets them know that they bear ultimate responsibility for their performance. *Take personal responsibility.*

- She serves the process. She controls what she can control, surrenders control of the rest, and detaches from the outcome, because it is not in her hands — it is not in anybody's hands — whether her team always wins or even whether it always plays well. *Have goals and faithfully serve them in a way that honors process.*

These are some of the hats that an athletic coach wears. If you decide to coach yourself, you will want to wear all these hats — and an existential fedora too. Why an "existential hat"? Because matters of meaning are of vital importance to you. An actor who can only find commercials to do, a writer grudgingly penning the eleventh mystery in a series, a painter who wakes up to discover that she no longer believes in her all-red canvases, a scientist who realizes that her corner of microbiology is producing nothing of interest are all ripe for a meaning crisis. A creativity self-coach works in the territory of personal meaning, and, if she practices, ultimately becomes a meaning expert.

Becoming a Meaning Expert

Are you good at judging when a project feels rich and meaningful to you and when it doesn't? Are you adept at maintaining meaning when your current work is routine, tedious, boring, obligatory, or just-for-hire? Are you aware when a meaning crisis has hit? Do you know how to shore up meaning leaks? Do you have a useful repertoire of meaning sparks, small things that you do to quickly restore meaning? In short, are you practiced at handling the meaning matters in your life?

Most people can't answer yes to any of these questions. Many aren't even aware of this territory, the territory of meaning. I suggest that you become aware and adept. Add to your creativity kit a notebook in which you reflect on meaning regularly and monitor the meaning issues in your life.

You write a decent short story. You send it out. Your story is rejected. You find the strength to send it out again. Again it is rejected. Again you send it out. Again it is rejected. This last rejection letter you reduce to ashes. Despair and anger set in. The next time you send your story out, you mail it in a dirty envelope and enclose an ironic cover letter. You don't enclose the stamped, self-addressed envelope you know you must include. You hear nothing. You are actually happy to be spared another rejection, and also devastated. You would kill someone if that didn't mean prison.

Hating the marketplace, you decide to write a "difficult" novel, a sly, convoluted affair that you know for dead certain will be wanted by no one. "Ha, ha!" you laugh. "I'll show them!" You spend a year writing your revenge novel and don't bother to send it out to agents or editors. Or if you do, it is with a vitriolic cover letter about the state of culture in America. "If you are looking for a bestseller, you won't find it here!" you proclaim. While your cover letter pleases you enormously, the subsequent silence is not quite so delicious.

This is what happens to a person with no self-coaching persona in place. Maybe the way you falter is by taking on one design job after another so as to avoid an encounter with your own imagery. Maybe your way is to labor on a single project for a decade, unable to complete it and to move on. Maybe your way is not to choose and not to commit. We each have our own way of faltering. Can you picture how much better it would be if you had a personal creativity coach in your life, one who was there to pat you on the back, treat your psychic wounds, and kick you in the butt?

You can become your own creativity coach. I've described the skills that you need to practice. There is nothing for you to complete in a day or a week, no deadline to meet, no final exam looming on the horizon. There is just the straightforward work of coaching yourself to higher creativity. You will thank yourself if you accept this challenge. There will be setbacks; there will be slips; there will be outright failures. Nobody who chooses to create is spared hurricanes and tornadoes. Only ask yourself this question: Is there any life you would rather lead than a creative one? If the answer is no, hire yourself on right now.

Brooklyn, New York

Fifty years ago, at the age of six, I moved with my mother from the Bronx to Brooklyn. At eighteen I enlisted in the army and left Brooklyn, essentially for good. I lived there again for several months when I was twenty-seven but in such a state of wackiness that I tend to discount that period as real. During those surreal months I stood at some brink, a brink two of my aunts had stepped over into mental institutions. A person who is blessed with a long life of creating is likely to come to this brink more than a few times, since the compulsion to create is not the only hammer banging in a creator's skull.

Take Paul, a former client of mine. His particular brink was the alcoholic's. On a regular basis Paul would throw up his hands and give himself permission to do really stupid things. He slid easily from ready drinker to alcoholic, routine carelessness to blackouts and broken legs, bohemian artist to bum. He would smash your car and borrow rent money from you if you let him. His demons ruled the roost, and his motto was "Screw everything!"

In his twenties he wrote poetry as obscure as Ezra Pound's, full of allusions to Byzantium and muffled cries for help. In his thirties, while drinking heavily, he married, divorced, and began drifting. He lived on the brink and then over it. He could certainly write; but one chaotic novel never got past page fifty, and a second ran to a thousand pages of digressions. People would say about Paul, "What a waste of talent!" What they ought to have said was, "What a waste of a life!"

One night, during his thirty-seventh year, he slipped on the ice in Boston. He was drunk and high, as usual, but as he lay on the pavement, stunned but unhurt, a hundred disconnected thoughts coalesced into his version of hitting bottom. What he heard himself say was, "This is unnecessary." He smiled, got up, and walked away from the brink. Nobody knows why such changes of heart happen, except that the person sprawled on the ice must play his part and get some of the credit.

It took Paul five years to stand up. He snared odd jobs, as a carpenter's assistant, a dog walker, a part-time gardener. He named his lifelong depression as such and made a conscious effort to side with life. His long walks were now in daylight rather than in the dead of night looking to score. Out of a superstitious worry that he was still very close to the brink, he never said outright, "I am a new man." But he was. To remind himself of where he had been he would mutter, "I could slip on the ice in the desert," a twist on a South American painter's phrase "I paint my deserts in the jungle."

Each day he thanked his lucky stars for a second chance at life. He constantly reminded himself that what he now had could be lost in the blink of an eye. He lived each day "one day at a time," the meaning of which he understood perfectly. He didn't write, but he readied himself to write. He readied himself by healing, by growing lucid, by practicing discipline, by showing courage. He married a professional woman for love. His disastrous early years could not be read in his countenance. He looked well and felt well.

The heartfelt novel that Paul wrote at forty-five, his first serious writing in a dozen years, was snapped up by the first literary agent to read it. Agitated by the agent's phone call, Paul's first impulse was to drink vodka. Instead he went for a long walk. By the time he got back, he had a smile on his face. He called the agent to accept her offer. She painted a beautiful picture of how large an advance he would receive for his brilliant novel. He smiled. It wasn't that he didn't believe her, although he didn't. He smiled because he hadn't taken a drink.

Paul had traveled to many far-flung places, but as a maniac. On his last trip before sobriety he'd done the dark side of Tangiers, Berlin, and Moscow, he'd scored on three continents, he'd eaten no square meals during months and months of desperate agitation. He wrote epic poems that, the morning after, turned out to be shopping lists. His Paris was the Paris of midnight, east of the Place de la République and in bed with swindlers. Although it did not really reflect who he was, he even carried a knife. That he could carry a knife even when he hated the idea of carrying one was proof positive that the life he was living was a complete mistake.

Sober, Paul returned to Paris for a visit. He stayed near the Eiffel Tower, away from his old haunts. He saw Paris in daylight for virtually the first time. There he began his second novel in the opposite of a frenzy, in a gentle way that belied the fact that he was generating tremendous power. You probably know that novel and not his first, which that agent never did sell. One day she called Paul to say that his novel had proven too difficult to sell and that she was through trying. He smiled again, although that smile didn't come easily.

Now that first novel actually will be easy to sell, given the success of his second novel, or so his new agent says. Paul isn't sure whether it will or not, and he can't waste time fantasizing or speculating. Not a Taoist, he is nevertheless attracted to Taoist poetry. The Taoist poets remind him that his job is to do what is appropriate for him to do. All the rest is so far out of his control that a serene smile is his only rational response. What is appropriate is that today he remain sober and that today he write.

I am staying in Manhattan and will meet Paul in Brooklyn tomorrow for a cup of coffee. It is storming and I picture my Brooklyn pounded by rain. I see factory yards full of plaster saints pummeled by the torrent, lightning flashing high in the sky above the Atlantic Ocean, crazy ladies in the halfway houses near Rockaway Beach watching the rain through fogged windows. Along Ocean Parkway the benches stand empty; the horse path, running all the way from Coney Island to Prospect Park, will have turned to mud. I stare out my Manhattan hotel window and see, not Ninth Avenue, which is directly below me, but the Brooklyn of 1954.

I began writing my first book, a novel, more than thirty years ago. Why? From what place is that spell cast? This morning I did the math and discovered that during those thirty years I'd written, edited, or compiled almost fifty books, journals, and decks. Three of those I ghostwrote. Three of those I self-published. Fifteen or more, mostly novels, were never published. Two dozen found their way into print. I have every story to tell, stories of abject failure and measured success, stories about the silly messes I made and the grown-up work I sometimes accomplished.

I think of those fifteen unpublished manuscripts. It is hard enough to contemplate one manuscript that you finished and didn't sell. But fifteen? Most of them date from the era of carbon paper and Wite-Out! If I were my own creativity coach — and I am — what would I advise? That I forget about them, even though some of them are juicy? That I pull one out, revise it, and offer it back up to the marketplace? Fifteen! I have to smile internally when a writer tells me that her first two novels haven't sold. I appreciate her pain and her disappointment, but still I have to smile. You have two manuscripts to mourn? I have fifteen!

Every unpublished manuscript is a problem, a tragedy, a waste, a dirty little secret. It is also part and parcel of the creative life. The five years you spent painting in a style you now find ridiculous is a problem, a tragedy, a waste, a dirty little secret. It is also part and parcel of the creative life. The performance of your play guaranteed to you by that repertory director who at the last minute reneged, the theory you worked on for nine years until you almost went blind that your rival at Princeton published three days before you finished your article, the — need I say more? These are our problems, our tragedies, our wastes, our dirty little secrets. We've had our hearts broken, and sometimes we've done our damnedest to break our own hearts. This is our life.

The next day a bright blue sky magically appears. It is chilly outside but gorgeous. I take the subway to Brooklyn. Paul and I meet at the Montague Street Plaza in Brooklyn Heights, a spot with world-famous views of the Manhattan skyline. You have been to this spot a thousand times without knowing it because of the countless print ads and movies that have employed this location. I used to pass by here at the age of seven on my way to first grade, in the days when the neighborhood landmark was the St. George Hotel. The St. George was home to the world's largest indoor swimming pool and had a pinball arcade overlooking the pool area. I would visit that arcade just about every morning on my way to school.

Paul appears in a long black coat, jeans, and boots, a Brooklyn Heights cowboy with a leathery face and hard edges who, as it happens, is carrying the *London Times Literary Supplement* and two containers of coffee. We divide up the paper to sit on, since the bench hasn't dried from yesterday's rain. I see that Paul has graduated to kid gloves, which he pulls off so as to enjoy the warmth of his coffee container.

"Beautiful day," I say.

"Splendid," Paul agrees.

We drink our coffee. To the right looms the Brooklyn Bridge. Far to the left is Lady Liberty. In front of us, larger than life and near enough to touch, is Manhattan. Paul and I catch up. We chat about writing and publishing. He tells me that his first novel has indeed sold, for a princely advance. I congratulate him. It will come out in a printing so large that he is embarrassed to say the number. We smile wryly; we know how many bottoms there are for every top. As we chat, I am aware that Paul isn't mentioning his current work. Finally he grows silent. I am positive what his silence signifies. Paul puts the lid back on his cup and readies himself.

"So," he says. "Can I tell you about the novel I'm writing? It's a total mess. It's a courtroom drama — that's probably the first mistake. What do I know about courtrooms? Every scene sounds like something I've heard or read before — "

I put down my coffee and give Paul my undivided attention. I know when a creativity coach is needed.

APPENDIX

CREATIVITY COACHING
AS A PROFESSION

C reativity coaching is a very young profession, one that I believe I invented out of whole cloth in the early 1990s. It remains to be seen whether or not it will become a viable full-time professional niche. Since the field of creativity coaching is so new, most creative people know nothing about it, not even that it exists. I believe that this will change, however, as more people enter this embryonic field and begin to work as practicing coaches. To date, hundreds of fledgling creativity coaches have trained with me and have begun practicing creativity coaching all over America and around the world.

What do creativity coaches do? They do exactly the work that I've been describing in this book, with their own style and flair. They help clients make and sustain meaning. They investigate issues of blockage, self-doubt, anxiety, fear of failure, worries about mistakes, and other issues that interfere with creating. They help creators deal with marketplace issues, career issues, issues of isolation and alienation, and other problems that inevitably arise for people who choose to create. They cheerlead, listen, educate, respond, and help their clients produce deeper work and adapt better to the realities of the world.

Creativity coaches also become much more effective self-coaches. The creativity coaches I train find it impossible not to look at their own creativity issues as they work with clients and think long and hard about what hinders creative expression. A coach-in-training begins to see why she never finished her mystery novel as she works with a blocked painter or composer. A coach-in-training discovers that her negative self-talk has caused her to stand on the creativity sidelines. Coaches-in-training learn that they can be of great help to their clients, and they also learn how to help themselves. In the course of our sixteen weeks together (via email) participants begin to understand, not abstractly or intellectually but personally and viscerally, what it takes to create.

My trainings are conducted via email so that people separated by vast geographic distances can work easily and effectively with one another. A creativity coach in Ireland can work with a client in Israel. A writer in Georgia and a painter in Delhi can work with the same creativity coach in Chicago. One of the many advantages of this cyberspace opportunity is that creativity coaches who could not possibly build a practice in their locale, because it is home to too few working artists, can build a practice by reaching out across the country and around the world.

We shall see if cyberspace will aid the growth of this new profession. What I know for certain is that the work we do as creativity coaches is soul stirring and vitally needed. If you are an artist, a helping professional like a therapist, a coach in some other discipline, a teacher, or anyone excited by the vision of supporting, educating, comforting, and coaching creative and would-be creative souls, I invite you to think about training with me. Visit my website at www.ericmaisel.com to find out more. I look forward to hearing from you and maybe having you come aboard.

Creativity coaching is the activity of one person helping another with the psychological, emotional, existential, and practical problems that arise as he or she tries to create. Virtually nothing is out-of-bounds as a creativity coach endeavors to help her client write, paint, invent, or compose and lead a rich life that centers around creating. I can't think of a more interesting or valuable vocation for a new century and a new millennium. It is beautiful work; it is needed work; it is one of the few new things under the sun. Last but not least, it is its own work of art. Come join us in the trenches and help us turn this fledgling profession into a real path with pay and heart.

RESOURCES

he following books of mine supplement the ideas
and strategies offered in *Coaching the Artist
Within.*

Affirmations for Artists (Tarcher, 1996). The affirmation process is
taught, two hundred issues of importance to creative individu-
als are identified and described, and an affirmation is provided
for each issue. Issues examined include achieving balance,
cultivating an audience, finding community, building confi-
dence, honing craft, surviving criticism, and maintaining discipline.

The Art of the Book Proposal: From Focused Idea to Finished Proposal (Tarcher, 2004). Explores the main elements of the nonfiction book proposal, the nonfiction writer's primary selling tool, and talks writers through the process of moving from a vague idea through the many changes that naturally occur until a focused book idea finally takes shape.

The Creativity Book: A Year's Worth of Inspiration and Guidance (Tarcher, 2000). Designed as a yearlong program of weekly lessons and exercises, *The Creativity Book* explores such vital issues as forgiveness and self-forgiveness, mindfulness, creative exploration, truthfulness, ambitiousness, discipline, risk-taking, resiliency, and planning and scheduling.

Deep Writing: Seven Principles That Bring Ideas to Life (Tarcher, 1999). Seven principles of importance to all creators are presented: hushing the mind, holding the intention to create, making creative choices, honoring the creative process, befriending one's creative work, evaluating one's creative work, and doing whatever is necessary to achieve and sustain a creative life.

Everyday Calm: 30 Ways to Soothe Your Inner Beast (Red Wheel, 2004). A set of easy-to-use reminders in deck form.

Everyday Creative: 30 Ways to Wake Up Your Inner Artist (Red Wheel, 2004). A set of easy-to-use reminders in deck form.

Everyday Smart: 30 Ways to Spark Your Inner Genius (Red Wheel, 2004). A set of easy-to-use reminders in deck form.

Fearless Creating: A Step-By-Step Guide to Starting and Completing Your Work of Art (Tarcher, 1995). An examination of the stages of the creative process — nurturing the wish to create, choosing creative projects, starting a project, working to completion, and showing and selling the work — with a focus on handling the particular anxieties associated with each stage. Many tips and exercises provided.

Fearless Presenting: A Performance Anxiety Workbook (Back Stage Books, 1997; revised, 2005). A complete program for handling performance anxiety, which is broadly defined to include the anxiety that wells up in a creator when she faces the blank canvas or the blank computer screen. Many techniques for managing performance anxiety are described, among them cognitive techniques, relaxation techniques, disidentification techniques, and guided visualizations.

A Life in the Arts: Practical Guidance and Inspiration for Creative and Performing Artists (Tarcher, 1994). An examination of the practical and emotional challenges that working artists face, organized into three interrelated areas: personality challenges, creative work challenges, and marketplace challenges ("personality, work, and world"). Many tips and exercises provided.

Living the Writer's Life: A Complete Self-Help Guide (Watson-Guptill, 1999). Subjects covered include a writer's work, a writer's education, a writer's craft, a writer's personality, a writer's challenges, a writer's strengths, a writer's relationships, a writer's world, and a writer's career. Provocative questions and solicited pieces from writers and editors (for instance, on the psychological relationship between editor and writer) highlight each chapter.

Sleep Thinking: The Revolutionary Program That Helps You Solve Problems, Reduce Stress, and Increase Creativity While You

Sleep (Adams Media, 2001). Presents an eighteen-step program for using deep (NREM) sleep as a time to solve problems, including creative ones, and argues that if creative people go to bed wondering about their work, they will wake up each morning ready to create. Supported by recent scientific evidence, the Sleep Thinking Program helps creative people hold the intention to create, increase their creative output, and deepen their work.

The Van Gogh Blues: The Creative Person's Path through Depression (Rodale, 2002). An investigation of the existential depression and meaning crises that regularly afflict creative people and strategies for handling these pernicious problems. Emphasis is put on the idea of creating as a meaning-making activity and what happens when a creative person can't make or maintain sufficient meaning.

Write Mind: 299 Things Writers Should Never Say to Themselves (and What They Should Say Instead) (Tarcher, 2002). A cognitive approach to overcoming writing blocks is presented in this book. Using the device of paired sentences, one a "wrong thing" that a writer might say to himself and the second the "right thing" he might prefer to say, writers are helped to understand how to identify and overcome negative and limiting self-talk.

A Writer's Paris: 60 Lessons from the City of Light (Writer's Digest Books, 2005). Lessons in the creative life set against a Parisian backdrop.

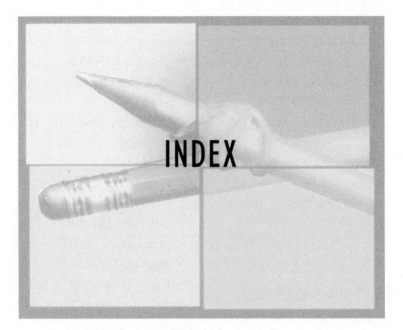

INDEX

passionately making meaning,
19–33
   vs. avoiding passion, 24–25
   deciding to matter, 19–20
   life purposes, holding
      intention to fulfill,
      23–26
   life purpose statements,
      20–22
   overview/components,
      19–22
   screenwriter case study,
      26–33
perfectionism, 140
performance anxiety, 42–43
personal vs. commercial art,
   59–60, 62
phone coaching, xvi
physical energy, 75–76, 77
Pippin, Aleta, 80–81
planning and doing, 159–74,
   196–97
   agreeing to plan, 161–65
   creating everyday/long-
      term plans, 165–67
   overview, 159–61
   theater case study,
      167–69, 171–74
positive obsessions, 78–82
process vs. product, 56–57
project logs, 194

R

reality testing, 175–76
   See also dreams and real-
      ity
regularity/routine, importance
   of, xviii–xix
resignation, 127
resistance, 190, 192
responsibility, 197
right thinking, 45
   See also wrong thinking
Rising Sun (Indiana) case
   study, 10–17
Ritalin, 75
Romance Writers of America,
   168–69
routine/regularity, importance
   of, xviii–xix
Russian Tea Room (New York
   City), 99

S

Saadi of Shariz, 50
Salmon, Paul, 42–43
San Francisco, 116–17
Savannah College of Art
   and Design (SCAD), 45–46
seemliness, 100
self-bashing, 35

ABOUT THE AUTHOR

Eric Maisel, PhD, is a licensed family therapist and creativity coach with a doctorate in counseling psychology and master's degrees in creative writing and counseling. A bestselling author, he has written more than twenty works of nonfiction and fiction, including *The Van Gogh Blues,* a finalist for the prestigious 2002 Books for a Better Life Award. He is a regular contributor to *Writer's Digest* and *The Writer* magazine and also pens the monthly "Psychology of Creativity" column for *Art Calendar* magazine.

Maisel maintains a private creativity coaching practice in San Francisco. He also trains creativity coaches and presents workshops on artists' issues nationally and internationally. For more information or to sign up for his free newsletter, please visit www.ericmaisel.com